JOHN MIDDLETON
Victorian, Provincial Architect

Brian E Torode

ACCENT
Zagreb, Croatia

Credits for illustrations:

The illustrations used are from the author's personal collection, with the following exceptions:

Hugh Greenhalf, Frontispiece, John Middleton
John Wheeler, Fig 11,12
Bill Fawcett, Fig 3,4,5,6,9,14 and 8 (John Mallon Collection)
The late Nigel Temple, 39,40,44,45
The Rev Canon Allan Maclean, 41,42,43

A more detailed and comprehensive version of this book, fully referenced and annotated can be seen at the following Centres:

Cheltenham Reference Library
Gloucestershire Archives
Darlington Library, Centre for Local Studies
Durham County Record Office
Borthwick Institute of Historical Research, York
National Library of Wales, Aberystwyth
Carmarthenshire Archive Service, Carmarthen
Cardigan Record Office, Aberystwyth
Pembrokeshire Record Office, Haverfordwest

A CIP catalogue record for this book is available from the National and University Library in Zagreb under No. 672136.

CIP zapis dostupan u računalnom katalogu Nacionalne i sveučilišne knjižnice u Zagrebu pod brojem 672136.

ISBN 978-953-99762-5-3

Cover illustration, Middleton's Westholme

Contents

J. Middleton.

Foreword

I have lived in Cheltenham for forty years and have been associated with St Stephen's Church, Tivoli, for most of that period. This church was designed by the architect, John Middleton in 1873 and when co-writing the history of the church to commemorate the centenary of the laying of the foundation stone in 1973, I was puzzled by the lack of information that I was able to access about Middleton the man. There were parish histories of some of his other Cheltenham churches and a reasonable amount of archival material covering St Stephen's in the county archives, but apart from this, I was not able to find anything that would help me to put flesh on the architect of five of Cheltenham's Victorian churches as well as Cheltenham Ladies' College.

What was known locally about Middleton was contained in a short book written by L. W. Barnard FRIBA, *Ninety Years Past, a History of the Office of L. W. Barnard and Partners.* This firm was the successor to that which had been started by Middleton in Cheltenham back in 1860.

While researching the St Stephen's Parish History in 1973, the colleague with whom I was working was able to borrow some Middleton archives – since deposited at Gloucestershire Archives– but these contained nothing about the man himself and at the time, anything that did not relate specifically to St Stephen's seemed irrelevant. After publication, my interest waned somewhat but any written or spoken information about John Middleton which came my way was filed for future reference. Gradually I built up a portfolio of his work and my interest was revived. Some sources were obvious, such as Pevsner's *Buildings of England* series, the RIBA archives, and eventually, the many plans and account books which had by that time, been deposited at the Gloucestershire Archives.

A chance reference to Middleton, found in a letter in the Centre for Local Studies in Darlington Library, enabled me to contact Bill Fawcett who was at the time researching railway architecture in the north-east of England. It is due in no small measure to his guidance and direction that I was able to build up a picture – albeit incomplete - of Middleton's work in the north of England.

Other leads soon followed and with the help of Thomas Lloyd of Cresselly, Pembrokeshire and the late Christopher Bishop who had worked with L. W. Barnard in Cheltenham, I was eventually able to discover more about John Middleton, "an obscure provincial architect" as Sir Hugh Casson once described him.

In 2002 John Morgan-Guy, the Archivist at University of Wales Lampeter, kindly invited me to contribute an essay entitled 'Middleton and St David's College, Lampeter', for a volume entitled *A bold imagining*, published to mark the 175th anniversary of Lampeter. That article seems to fittingly acknowledge Middleton's contribution to the Anglican renaissance that took place in South Wales during the closing decades of the nineteenth century.

I hope that the story which follows will promote interest in one of those many provincial architects whose work is not of national significance, but who made important contributions to the architectural heritage of the towns in which they lived and practised.

Brian Torode 2008

Acknowledgements

As with any research of this nature, numerous persons and organisations have provided help and support in a variety of ways. The majority of organisations to which I have resorted for archives or help with locating buildings are all acknowledged in the references at the end of this book. However I do want to thank the staff of all these establishments for the cheerful and willing way in which they have encouraged me and gone to immense trouble to help me solve, interpret and sort the many puzzling and challenging pieces of evidence which have been examined over the course of many years.

Many individuals too have shared the fruits of their own research and shared with me photographs, newspaper cuttings, personal memories and suggestions for further avenues of research. In some cases, I have been welcomed into the homes of strangers and received hospitality from people whom I had previously known only through correspondence.

Research that covers such a wide geographical area has entailed much travel and I have been fortunate to have had the help of Richard Barton who has frequently acted as chauffeur and navigator on excursions to many unfamiliar places. I have often relied on him for help with interpreting plans and drawings and relating these to the actual buildings. He has also been instrumental in proof reading and editing the text of this book.

At the end of the text, I have acknowledged individuals at local level who have made my research profitable, interesting and above all rewarding. To any whom I have inadvertently omitted, my profound apologies, and sincere thanks.

I also wish to place on record my debt of gratitude to Professor Barry Davies of the Business School, University of Gloucestershire, for his invaluable help in arranging for the publication of this Biography of John Middleton.

I would welcome any corrections or additions to the information contained in this study of the life and work of John Middleton. I accept full responsibility for any inaccuracies contained in this text, assuring readers that what has been produced has been done in good faith, based on material evidence available at the time of publication.

Introduction

Very little has been written about the life and career of John Middleton, although in recent times there has been a growing interest in the man and his work especially in Cheltenham, a town which boasts five Victorian Gothic churches built to his designs. This book does not claim in any way to be an architectural or scholarly appreciation of Middleton's work. It is a record of his life and his contribution to Victorian, provincial architecture.

John Middleton has received due recognition in Pevsner's *The Buildings of England* series but this has been confined, as one would expect, to an acknowledgement of his work rather than to biographical details. Few people realise the extent to which he travelled in pursuit of his career and little published information about him is available even in the main areas in which he practised – the north-east of England, Gloucestershire and Wales. Hopefully this account will introduce the reader to the variety of contracts on which he was engaged and at the same time, paint a written portrait of a man who adopted Cheltenham as his home and to whom the town owes some of its most prominent Victorian buildings.

CHAPTER I

John Middleton's early years

Although John Middleton spent most of his working life in Cheltenham, he was not a native of Gloucestershire. In fact, John Middleton was a true Yorkshireman, born in the city of York on 27th August 1820 at 90, Lower Goodramgate. His baptism followed at Holy Trinity Church, Goodramgate, on 5th September of that year. His father Thomas had also been baptised there in January 1774, the son of George and Catherine Middleton of Delpike Parish. John's mother, Hannah Sowersby came from Sculcoates near Hull and she and Thomas were married in St Cuthbert's Church, York, in May 1806. John Middleton's birthplace still stands today, in one of the oldest parts of York, and is the tea rooms for the National Trust next door to the Trust's shop. John was only thirteen years of age when his father died after a severe illness at the age of fifty-nine. *The Yorkshire Gazette* of 23rd November 1833 carried an obituary in which he was described as "a shopkeeper, an active parishioner, a good neighbour, an affectionate husband, a tender parent and respected by all who knew him," a fitting tribute to someone who had been admitted Freeman of the City of York in February 1798 after a seven year apprenticeship. Thomas had made his will three months before his death and in it he made provision for his dear wife Hannah Middleton and for "my only son, John Middleton until he attain the age of twenty-one years." Provision was also made for John should Hannah die before he reached his majority. In such circumstances, the executors were empowered to use all available funds to clothe, maintain and educate him until he reached the age of twenty-one. The executors, whose services were in-

Fig. 1 York, Holy Trinity, the Font.

deed called upon, were Thomas' brother-in-law John Sowersby and Caleb Williams, a surgeon of Micklegate in the City of York. The value of the estate was under £800, equating to probably £60,000 in today's terms.

John continued to live with his mother and his uncle in Goodramgate, until 25th October 1834 when the *Yorkshire Gazette* announced that "Mrs Hannah Middleton, relict of the late Thomas, flour dealer of Goodramgate," had died. At the age of just fourteen John Middleton was orphaned and his uncle John Sowersby became his legal guardian. The years after the death of his parents must have been difficult for young John, but his uncle was true to the wishes expressed in his father's will and ensured that he received a sound education. Up to the age of fifteen he was a pupil at Mr Monkman's private preparatory school in College Street, almost behind his home and near the east end of York Minster. When he was fifteen and a half years old, he transferred to the York Collegiate School. The school register for this period records the following details of his time at the school:

> Middleton, John, (15) Ref: 1/214
> 8 February 1836 – Midsummer 1838
> Lives with Mr Sowerby (sic) Goodramgate, York.
> Previously at Mr Monkman's School, York.

Fees were £10 per annum and hours were long. In February 1838 the school moved to a new site at Clifton where John spent his final two terms, leaving at the age of eighteen in Midsummer of that year. It would seem that immediately on leaving school, John entered the office of James Pigott Pritchett as a pupil architect. The office was only a short distance from Goodramgate and the usual apprenticeship at that period lasted five years. No doubt his father's provision for his education covered the payment of fees but

Fig. 2 York, Middleton's birthplace.

from 1841, he inherited the trust set up for him by his father, and he would then have been able to pay his own pupilage premium from that time onwards. Architects of the period did not have to work towards examinations for recognised qualifications but they qualified on recommendation and the merits of their work. The Institute of British Architects had only been founded, in 1834, and became "Royal" in 1837. In the early years one became a Member by nomination and subsequent election.

Middleton's mentor, James Pigott Pritchett was born in Pembrokeshire in 1789. By 1808 he was articled to the architect James Medland in Southwark. He later spent two years with the "brilliant and successful Daniel Asher Alexander," architect to the London Dock Company. Pritchett exhibited at the Royal Academy in 1808 and 1809 and began practice in London in 1812. He soon moved to York where he worked in partnership with Charles Watson just outside Micklegate Bar. The partnership was dissolved after eighteen years when at the age of forty-two, Pritchett opened his own office at 13, Lendal, York.

Pritchett was a member of a strict non-conformist Calvinist congregation and he and his wife Peggy were founder members of the York congregation. He designed their chapel at Lendal during his partnership with Watson, and it was opened in 1816. Pritchett and his wife Peggy had three sons and a daughter, Maria, who became Mrs John Middleton in 1844. Pritchett's first wife died in 1827 but he remarried two years later. Of this marriage three sons and two daughters were born. One of the sons, also named James Pigott Pritchett, was to feature in the early architectural career of John Middleton. Pritchett senior took on two of his sons as pupils, James and Charles, and other pupils whom he encouraged in their profession included Walter Blackett, J.C. Gilbert, Samuel Whitfield Daukes, James Medland junior and of course John Middleton. Of these, four came south and worked in the Gloucester-Cheltenham area. Daukes was working there as early as 1834, Medland later joined him as his chief assistant, Middleton arrived in Cheltenham much later, in 1859, and Pritchett's son Charles was working from Wotton-under-Edge by 1860.

No doubt, as a pupil, Middleton would have accompanied Pritchett on site visits to his many projects in the counties of north-east England and Pritchett likewise would have supervised his pupils during their work on projects which he had entrusted to them. Eventually the time came for John Middleton to take advantage of all that he had learnt, to leave the security of the Pritchett office and to set up in practice on his own, in Darlington.

Sources consulted:

University of York, Borthwick Institute of Historical Research, York. *Borthwick Texts and Calendars 18.*

Mitchell, John V, Archivist, St Peter's School, Clifton, York.

Dixon, Roger and Muthesius, Stefan: *Victorian Architecture.*

York City Archives.

York Institute of Architectural Study – *Studies in Architectural History Vol.II.* 1956.

York Reference Library.

York Probate Registry.

Pevsner, N: *The Buildings of England, Yorkshire and the North Riding.*

Colvin, Howard: *Dictionary of British Architects.*

CHAPTER II

The Beginning of the Practice

John Middleton appears to have started his architectural practice in Darlington in 1843 at a time when the town was developing as an important railway centre. This may have been one of the incentives to move from York, but he may equally have been encouraged by the presence there since 1840, of his future brother-in-law, Richard Charles Pritchett who was Minister to the Protestant Dissenters in the town. Middleton enjoyed a certain amount of financial security through the trust which his father had set up for him and which he inherited in 1841. Funds made available from this source may have been used to start his practice. On the other hand, he may have been partially assisted by James Pigott Pritchett, his mentor and future father-in-law, for on 10th July 1844 his daughter Maria married John Middleton at Lendal Chapel, York. The ceremony was performed by Maria's brother the above mentioned Richard, with her father James and Caleb Williams, one of the executors of Thomas Middleton's estate, as witnesses. Whatever the exact date of John Middleton's move to Darlington, the *Newcastle Chronicle* carried the following advertisement on 2nd March 1844:

> Workmen desirous of giving tenders for various works required in building a RESIDENCE etc at Ayton near Stokesley for Thomas Richardson esq. may see PLANS and SPECIFICATIONS at the Gas House Office, Middlesbrough, from Tuesday morning, 5th to Saturday evening 9th March, and at my office from Tuesday morning 12th to Saturday evening 16th March.
> J Middleton, Architect, Darlington. February 27th 1844.

The client, Thomas Richardson, had been born in Darlington in 1771 and became a wealthy and influential member of the Society of Friends. He was well connected through marriage to the railway developer, Edward Pease who was his cousin, and invested heavily in the Stockton and Darlington Railway. He was one of its original directors and partnered George and Robert Stephenson and Edward Pease in the former's locomotive works in Newcastle. Having extensive Quaker connections in the area, it is more than probable that Richardson was also well known to Caleb Williams, one of the executors of Thomas Middleton's will. He

Fig. 3 Thomas Richardson

was a Quaker, a surgeon and as enthusiastic about Quaker education of children as Richardson himself was. Caleb Williams therefore may well have been responsible for obtaining for Middleton his first identifiable commission.

Thomas Richardson was a very successful businessman and in 1830 he was able to retire from London and make a new home in Ayton where he had family connections. He initially took out a lease on Ayton House, which was quite near to where his cousins, the Hesletons lived, but due to a rather bitter dispute with the owner of the property over some tree felling, the lease was not renewed when it expired in 1842. Richardson did not want to move away from the area and began searching for land on which to build a house for himself, his wife having died by this time. Eventually he took possession of Sand Hill Field in June 1844 and plans for a new house on the site were immediately prepared by Middleton, contracts being signed within a matter of weeks. In less than a year the house was adequately habitable. A few rooms were hurriedly decorated and furnished and Richardson was able to leave the temporary accommodation he had secured in the village. The naming of the new property presented a challenge as the word Ayton was already being used in several house names in the village, and eventually Cleveland Lodge was decided upon. Richardson did not enjoy many years in his new home, for he died in April 1853 while on holiday at Redcar. In his will he left the house to two cousins and they made their home there.

Cleveland Lodge, a Grade II Listed Building, still stands today very much as Middleton designed it, on high ground east of the town of Ayton. It is a typical country villa of two storeys and five bays in sandstone ashlar. The house has a hipped roof, good classical detailing and a solid porch with square columns. The three-bay garden

Fig. 4 Cleveland Lodge

Fig. 5 Cleveland Lodge

front has a large central one-storey bow window and the north return has a small bell-cote which is still in working order. The two-storey wing to the east for servants was probably added to Middleton's original design at a later date. This was quite an important undertaking for a newly qualified architect and it no doubt served as a recommendation for his second commission in Ayton.

The Society of Friends was anxious to establish a school in the north-east in which children of Quaker parentage would receive an education which was in accordance with the Christian ethos of the Society of Friends. Thomas Richardson promised to donate £5000 towards the purchase of a suitable site in the Ayton area on which to build such a school. Philip Hesleton, a linen manufacturer and Richardson's cousin, decided to sell his 74 acre estate in the town and by 1841 work had been completed on the conversion of the handsome Georgian house, its mill and several cottages, all of which adjoined the Friends Meeting House. George Dixon was immediately appointed the first Headmaster of this "Quaker Agricultural School for the North of England." The architect of the conversion was a William Holmes of Newcastle. However Richardson was not entirely satisfied with boys and girls sharing the facilities which the school provided, and in 1846, shortly after the completion of Cleveland Lodge, he employed Middleton to produce plans for "new buildings for all the necessary purposes connected with kitchen, laundry, and dormitory for the boys." Middleton's main work for the school was a large block in dressed stone which looked very institutional indeed, the belfry of which bears the inscribed date 1846. Letters exist in the school's archives to suggest that Middleton had to sort out serious problems with the contractors – "I found a series of false charges and mischarges. Half the amount would be ample remuneration for the work done...I will meet the contractor to give his explanation."

To celebrate the school's fiftieth anniversary in 1891, George Dixon wrote the history of the school and a bronze medal was struck showing the original Ayton School in the centre and the Middleton block of 1846 to the left. It was great delight for the present author to visit Ayton in 2000 and to meet a former Ayton School matron, Miss Cumbor, who possesses one of these medals. The burial ground of The Friends' Meeting House alongside the school buildings contains the gravestone of Thomas Richardson as well as a wall mounted memorial stone. The school closed in 1998 and the buildings have undergone extensive conversion into domestic accommodation and now form the nucleus of a most attractive private estate set in ornamental grounds.

Sources consulted:

Fawcett, Bill: description of Cleveland Lodge.

Listed Buildings Description 23.6.66. Cleveland Lodge.

University of York, Borthwick Institute of Historical Research, York. *Borthwick Texts and Calendars 18.*

Jubilee History of ***Ayton School*** 1891.

Centenary History of Ayton School 1941.

North Yorkshire County Record Office, Northallerton: Ayton School Records, Ref ZFA.

Miss Cumbor, formerly of Ayton School.

O'Sullivan, Dan: *Great Ayton, A History of the Village,* 1983.

CHAPTER III

Middleton's work in and around Darlington

On arrival in Darlington, Middleton established himself at number 85 Bondgate, a premises which provided a business address and later a home for himself and his wife and son. In the early days he probably worked without assistants, apart from a clerk of works. Much of his time would have been taken up on site visits frequently involving overnight absence from home. His first local work would appear to be that for the Stockton and Darlington Railway Board, which in August 1844 recorded that the services of John Middleton were being harnessed in the conversion of a warehouse for the Company. Later in that same year, he signed a contract to render professional assistance to the Company, for which he would be paid an annual retainer - fifty guineas in the first year - plus expenses and free rail travel. This contract lasted until 1849 and must have seemed very attractive providing as it did, an assured annual income, small though it might seem by today's standards. Most of the work would have been routine repairs, alterations, additions and the solving of structural problems, although he would have worked closely with the Company's engineer when planning more specialised buildings. As the Company grew it sponsored other companies to build new lines and these eventually amalgamated with the Stockton and Darlington. This was good news for Middleton and between 1845 and 1849 he became architect to three such projects.

The Wear and Derwent Railway crossed a high exposed stretch of the Durham Moors and Middleton was accorded the task of building a new railway village at Waskerley. He designed homes for the several dozen workers and their families as well as some social amenities. He also designed engine sheds and repair shops. In the year 2000 the railway had long gone, only two or three of Middleton's buildings were still standing and those were in a very advanced state of disrepair.

Not far from Darlington is the town of Middlesbrough which in Middleton's time was a reasonably new and developing town. A dock was opened in 1842 specifically to handle coal traffic and Middleton's contribution to this initiative was the design of a dockside clock tower in 1847. A more impressive project in Middlesbrough however was the design of the railway station itself. This was a passenger station at the foot of Sussex Street and replaced an earlier one on another site near the riverbank. The foundation stone was laid in 1846 and the station was opened in July 1847. It was built of stone and brick. It had a portico with a pair of arches flanking the main entrance which was framed by a pair of Ionic columns. Local developers questioned the wisdom of such a large building so far from the town and the opinion of the residents was that

Fig. 6 Middleton's Middlesbrough Station, a reconstruction by Bill Fawcett

it was a rather pretentious edifice. In view of Middleton's later move to Cheltenham, it is interesting to note that the station which one sees today replaced Middleton's building in 1877 and was designed by Mr. William Peachey, who was born in Cheltenham but who had moved to Darlington!

The year 1846 also saw the opening of the Middlesbrough to Redcar Line, a development which had been requested by the residents of Redcar. They saw it as necessary to maintaining the popularity of the town as a resort as well as being to its commercial advantage. The whole project took eight months to complete and cost £36,000. Middleton was responsible for designing the elegant terminus and office buildings and a contemporary visitors' guide described the proposed station as a large, handsome building, "designed by Mr. Middleton of Darlington, which will not be an ornament, but of great public utility to the place, particularly by providing a large room eighty feet long, thirty feet wide, an accommodation which has hitherto been much required, as a promenade and place of public resort. Refreshment rooms are attached, and a capacious stone balcony will enable the invalid and the lounger to inhale the fresh sea breeze and to enjoy the prospect over the estuary of the Tees towards Hartlepool and the southern part of the County of Durham on the one hand, and over a boundless expanse of ocean studded with busy sails on the other."

This station was neo classical in design and constructed almost entirely of stone with a hipped roof and elegant tripartite windows, but the additional facilities originally envisaged were not completed at the same time. The *Newcastle Courant* for January 21st 1848 carried the following advertisement:

> "To Builders: persons desirous of giving tenders for the erection of an hotel and Promenade Room at Redcar may see the plans and specifications at my office from Monday 24th to Saturday 29th January, and at Redcar Station from Monday 31st to Wednesday 9th February 1848. J. Middleton, Architect, Darlington."

This obviously refers to the large Promenade Room mentioned in the visitors' guide, but further contemporary descriptions of the building indicate its fate. "The station is at the west end of the village and is not only useful for the purpose for which it was built but is also exceedingly ornamental. A large building was erected near to the station for a Promenade Room, but unfortunately was destroyed by fire before it was finished. It is now used as a warehouse." The hotel also referred to did not materialise due to a period of recession and Middleton was 'paid off' with £75 for his plans. The Company did not employ an architect again until 1853.

None of Middleton's stations survives along this line, but at Kirkleatham one can still admire a small terrace of railway cottages which he designed for Redcar in 1847. When the line was re-routed and the original station was closed in 1861, the cottages were dismantled and re-erected just west of Kirkleatham Church, in a small estate village just outside Redcar. The cottages are of yellow brick with sandstone dressings and bear the date 1847. They provide a beautifully maintained memorial to his railway contributions in this area, although one of the occupants complained to the author that "he could have made the rooms a bit higher!"

The Wear Valley Railway was authorised to extend westwards between 1845-1847 and Middleton was commissioned to design various stations along this line. Three still exist, although not serving the purpose for which they were originally built. Wolsingham, now a listed building, was a private home in 2000; Frosterley, in the Tudor gothic style, had been converted into a Nursery School and Witton-le-Wear, very much like Frosterley with a similar bay window, stood unoccupied but in good state of repair. Each bears a date shield for 1847.

Although his railway work provided a steady income in his early years as an architect in Darlington, John Middleton was responsible for other more exciting and lucra-

Fig. 7 Kirkleatham Cottages

Fig. 8 Wolsingham Station

Fig. 9 Frosterley Station

tive commissions, which allowed more imaginative and creative expression of his professional skills. An ever-increasing number of railway workers around the Bank Top Station area of Darlington presented many challenges to the York and Newcastle Railway Company. Matters of concern ranged from the provision of housing and public services to providing accommodation for worship. The latter concern was first addressed through making available a warehouse for Sunday worship until such time as a church could be provided. In July 1845 a new ecclesiastical district was created by Order in Council and included all that part of the parish of St Cuthbert, Darlington, to the east of the River Skerne - the railway workers' district. George Hudson, the 'Railway King' was adamant that any new church must be conspicuous and attractive, and subscriptions were invited towards the erection of a new place of worship.

The Newcastle Courant of 4th June 1847 carried an invitation to contractors,

> "desirous of building a church at Bank Top, Darlington, to inspect the drawings and specifications at my office, Monday 7th to Wednesday 16th June next.
> J. Middleton, Architect, Darlington."

Fig. 10 Darlington, St John

The foundation stone of the Church of St John the Evangelist was laid on Friday 10th September that same year, although work had already started. Voluntary contributions towards the estimated cost of £3,200

Fig. 11 Darlington, St John

amounted to £2,500 and George Hudson in his speech, said that he hoped the church would be opened without debt, and that "no female will feel that she is performing her duty either to herself or to her family or to her husband if she is not seen in a place of worship on a Sunday."

Fig. 12 Darlington, St John

Although the church had been completed by 1849, it was not until January 1850 that the official opening took place. *The Darlington and Stockton Times* heaped lavish praise upon the architect –"The credit of the architectural department is due to J. Middleton esq. to whose untiring attention much of the elegance of the building is owing." The final cost amounted to £4000 and the church provided seating for over 630 worshippers, of which 389 sittings were free. The church is in the Early English style of architecture and makes an impressive contribution to the Darlington skyline, standing as it does in a prominent position overlooking the town. The strong square tower was built to support a spire of 160 feet but like four of Middleton's later churches in Cheltenham, money was just not forthcoming. The original pulpit, richly arcaded and carved from Caen stone was the architect's gift to the church, but the present one is a replacement of 1890. However the existing font is the original one. The church stands today largely unaltered and internally, the roof and the sanctuary's Minton encaustic tiles are worthy of close inspection. Plans were also prepared for a Vicarage, to the designs of Middleton and Pritchett, and it was completed in 1856, although probably under the supervision of Middleton's partner and brother-in-law, James Pigott Pritchett junior.

Fig. 13 Central Hall, Darlington

Further work in Darlington included the Central Hall, the National Bank of England, and the construction of an exhibit for the 1851 Great Exhibition. The Central Hall was built as Darlington's cultural centre in 1846, and was opened in June 1847 to provide an alcohol-free meeting place for the town. The internal planning was described at the time as being superior to any other

Fig. 14 High Row Bank, Darlington.

provision in the town. The overall cost was £6,000 funded by a consortium of Quaker shareholders. The stone commemorative lintel still exists, adorning the window at one side of the present remodelled building. Not far away, on High Row, Darlington, stood a branch of the National Provincial Bank of England. A decision was made in 1849 to upgrade the building which stood on a narrow site between two other buildings and Middleton was engaged to carry out the work. *The Civil Engineer and Architects' Journal* for December 1850 introduced its evaluation of Middleton's design by stating that although it was not one of the more ambitious of its class it was nevertheless "a very good example of the application of moderate resources and we are happy to have this opportunity of giving proof to his successful application." *The Builder,* however, was less than flattering in its comments about the appropriateness of the design for the town-"(The building) appears to be a rather stylish sort of edifice for such a place as Darlington."

Fig. 15 High Row Bank, Darlington..

In 1851 there was on show at the Central Hall, a model of York Minster made by John Middleton, prior to being taken to the Crystal Palace for display at the Great Exhibition. The model was almost three feet in length and constructed on a scale of fifteen feet to the inch. The windows were decorated to represent stained glass and the model could be illuminated from inside. It was made of white cardboard and received much praise from both the local press and *The Ecclesiologist*, the journal of the Cambridge Camden Society.

By the late 1840s Middleton was well established in Darlington. As we already know, his brother-in-law Richard Pritchett was the Congregational minister in the town until 1850. No doubt this added to Middleton's credibility amongst the non-conformists, especially the Quakers, although his purchase of a sizeable shareholding in the West Auckland Brewery Company in 1845 may have caused some raised eye-brows. He later became a shareholder in the North Bitchburn Coal Company and in May 1850 he was one of a consortium of thirteen local businessmen who offered them-selves as surety for the provision and development of the first park and recreation ground for the town. This involvement in local affairs and the attention given to his work in local and architectural publications added greatly to his professional profile in the area and were to prove useful points of reference in the future as we shall see when we later consider the second phase of his career in Cheltenham.

Sources consulted:

Bill Fawcett for Middleton's **railway contributions.**

Ken Hoole Railway Study Centre, Darlington.

Teesside Archives, Middlesbrough Local Studies Library, Ref MM1712.5.

Middlesbrough Borough Council: *Middlesbrough's Heritage, The World's First Railway Town.*

Wheeler, John, and Moat, Neil, for **St John's Church**, Darlington.

The Ecclesiologist Vol 12.

Darlington and Stockton Times, 3.1.1850 and 23.9.1853; St John's Church.

Church of England: Council for the Care of Churches.

University of Durham Library: CCP AI/5(temp) **St John's Parsonage**, Darlington.

Mrs Vera Chapman for Darlington's Victorian Architects and St John's Vicarage

Kelly's Directory for 1921; St John's Vicarage.

Aspects of Darlington – WEA publication.

Durham County Record Office, County Hall: DX 1264/1-3 and D/NBCC 2/13

Listed Building Description, **Central Hall**, Grade II 17.8.72.

Darlington Library, Centre for Local Studies.

The Builder. 7.9.1850. **The High Row Bank.**

The Civil Engineer and Architects' Journal December 1850.

CHAPTER IV

Further work in the north-east. Middleton as mentor

Most of the commissions that we have looked at so far have been for new buildings, but Middleton also undertook much work that involved restoration or alteration of existing buildings. Several such commissions were small in comparison with Cleveland Lodge, the Central Hall or St John's Church, but the available correspondence and plans show that he gave as much professional attention to detail with these as he did to the more impressive work that he undertook.

Coniscliffe is just a short distance from Darlington and the former vicarage occupies a very dramatic setting, squeezed in as it is between the grounds surrounding the church and a steep, cliff face overlooking a deep valley below. A new vicar, the Reverend Henry Baumgartner was appointed to the parish in 1849 and was presented with a vicarage which had been seriously neglected by his predecessor. Middleton was immediately engaged to examine the building with a view to carrying out necessary repairs and structural alterations. A faculty to carry out the work was granted and Middleton's drawings and specifications are good examples of his meticulous attention to detail. His plans included the rebuilding of a wing to the west side of the house, renewal of the roof and some flooring, and the rebuilding of several outbuildings. The work was completed to his specification by the end of 1851 but later additions were made in 1860 to the designs of the architect S. S. Teulon. Middleton's part of the house was demolished in 1967 but is clearly visible on a postcard c1907. The former vicarage is now a private house.

Fig. 16 Hartlepool, Holy Trinity

At the same time, but further afield, the town of Hartlepool was developing as a coal shipping port and the rapid increase in the population made additional church accommodation desirable. A site was provided by the trustees of the late Duke of Cleveland on the western part of The Headland, the site of the medieval walled town and the 'new church' committee commissioned a design from Middleton which was subsequently accepted. The Mayor of Hartlepool laid the foundation stone of Holy Trinity Church on 20th August 1850. The church was in the Decorated or Middle Pointed style of architecture with a chancel, nave, north and south aisles and north and south porches. Like its counterpart in Darlington, the roof was of bold but simple design producing a most beautiful effect and the use of Minton tiles for the sanctuary added to the overall interior richness. A tower was planned but due to lack of immediate funding, this was put on hold. As a temporary measure a small bell gable was erected at the west end to accommodate two bells which were in place for the opening of the church in March 1852. Middleton was also commissioned to design a parsonage for the incumbent, the Reverend L. Paige. The thirty-three plans and the specifications were signed by Middleton and his brother-in-law and partner James Pigott Pritchett junior, but correspondence dated 1855 would suggest that the parsonage had not yet been built and no memories of it exist today. Holy Trinity Church was demolished in the early 1950s when it was suffering from major structural faults.

Between 1850 and 1855, John Middleton was responsible for the major refurbishment of All Saints Church, Manfield, south-west of Darlington and just over the County Durham border in Yorkshire. The church dates from the twelfth century and has a sixteenth century tower. The restoration and reordering were commissioned by the Lord of the Manor, Richard Bassett Wilson. Much of the lengthy and complicated correspondence between him and the incumbent, the Reverend Mr. Swire is still available to researchers. Middleton's initial plans were not acceptable to the Bishop of Ripon, and Middleton was forced to revise much of the work he had hoped to complete. However the Lord of the Manor, Mr. Wilson, questioned how far the diocesan authorities could dictate what could and could not be done, provided that the building was not in any way damaged. He considered Middleton's plans to be so well calculated so as to provide not only a neat but also a substantial building and in view of the attitude of the diocese, he withdrew his promise of a substantial contribution towards the restoration. The Bishop thereafter had a change of heart and agreed to most of the architect's proposals and this persuaded Mr. Wilson to honour his original offer. The 1849 estimates included a new oak and lead roof, new window glass, damp proofing of the walls, new clerestory windows, new tracery to the east window, new porch and doors, and many new internal furnishings. An additional estimate was provided in 1850 for a Rood Screen but this was one aspect of the work which was not realised. This project involved the architect in a heavy restoration of an ancient church and must have aroused some controversy and much interest amongst the local population, although no mention is made of the restoration in the journal of the Ecclesiological Society. This is surprising as Middleton's reordering of the interior accorded one hundred per cent with the principles of that learned Society.

Between 1844 and 1855 Middleton must have been involved with many projects some of which still wait to be identified. To date, no definite identification of Middleton's 1847 work at Neasham Hill, a large house east of the village of Neasham on the banks of the river Tees, has been possible although an advertisement inviting tenders appeared in the *Newcastle Courant* at that time. However it is probable that his partner, James Pigott Pritchett junior, later completed the major alterations to the house as he was responsible for the restoration of the neighbouring church in 1876 and the house owners were the Patrons of the Living. Additional newspaper reports and invitations to builders to tender for contracts also inform us of several other projects in this area undertaken by Middleton. These include, in 1848, minor additions to the school at Hurworth, the neighbouring village to Neasham, although Pritchett built a new school for the village in the 1870s. Middleton was also responsible for the building of an inn at Witton-le-Wear in 1846 and submitted a design for the rebuilding of Cockermouth Church in 1852. The latter plans were highly commended by the judges although in this instance, Middleton was unsuccessful.

Several references have been made above to Middleton's partner and brother-in-law, James Pigott Pritchett junior. He was younger than Middleton by ten years and served his apprenticeship with his father James Pigott Pritchett senior in York before moving first to Huddersfield where his father had a branch office, and then to Darlington to join Middleton. The earliest evidence we have for his presence in Middleton's office is a joint signature on the plans for the Hartlepool Vicarage in 1854, and *The Newcastle Courant* for July 25th 1855 carried an invitation to builders to tender for two Chapels at Jesmond Burial Ground to the design of Middleton and Pritchett, Architects, 85, Bondgate, Darlington.

The importance of architectural competitions at this time has already been addressed and there are several references to 'first premium' awards to the Middleton-Pritchett partnership. One such award was for St Nicholas Church, Durham, in 1854, although the work was actually completed by Pritchett alone in 1858, by which time Middleton had left Darlington. Partnership designs for Newcastle Cemetery and Saffron Walden Cemetery both gained first premiums, but an 1856 design for Darlington Cemetery was awarded a first premium in the name of Pritchett only. This may give some indication of Middleton's gradual withdrawal from the partnership, a probability supported by an affidavit sworn by Pritchett relating to Hartlepool Vicarage in 1855:

> "I James Pigott Pritchett of Darlington, do certify...that my ***late*** partner, Mr Middleton has drawn the plans and made the specifications."

This suggests that by 1855 Middleton was no longer a partner in the firm, but this assumption is further complicated by work done between 1855 and 1856 at St John the Baptist Church, Greatham. The work which consisted of an enlargement of the church to the designs of Middleton was most probably supervised by Pritchett. Middleton had been consulted early in 1850 with a view to increasing the seating capacity of the church which had been rebuilt on its Saxon foundations in 1792. First proposals suggested demolishing the tower at the west end and extending the church in that direction. This was considered too drastic a measure and received strong objections from local, influential benefactors. Revised plans eventually provided for the rather long chancel to be shortened at its west end by one bay, and the nave was extended eastwards into the newly created space by the addition of a pair of Romanesque piers and arches to the existing arcades. Sadly the interesting Norman chancel arch was pulled down and sold and replaced by a weak early English one, four paces eastward of the original. The 'new' church was opened for worship in March 1855 and although it has been suggested above that Middleton left the partnership around 1855, a letter exists written to the incumbent of St John the Baptist, from the architects' practice address in October 1857. The letter from Middleton congratulated him that "in my absence, the proposed work has been completed, I hope to your satisfaction. I beg to mention my account for plans etc. connected with the enlargement of the church, and shall be much obliged by a cheque for the amount." It would therefore appear that having prepared the plans in 1851, Middleton was then absent from Darlington for some time, and had probably delegated supervision of the contract to Pritchett.

As with the work at Manfield, that at Greatham must have aroused considerable interest and comment, especially over the destruction of the Norman chancel arch, but again, surprisingly, no comment is recorded in the journal of the Ecclesiological Society.

No details have been found for Middleton's whereabouts between 1855 and December 1857 apart from the fact that in that month, John Middleton, his wife and son John Henry, are included in the 'Arrivals List' in Torquay, where they stayed at 2, Higher Terrace until 26th May 1858. From there he corresponded with previous clients and gave Pritchett's Darlington address as a forwarding address. This does suggest that Middleton retained some interest in the partnership and that it had not been dissolved due to any ill-will.

During his years in Darlington, Middleton received pupils who came to him for training. They would accompany him on site visits, and he would have delegated to them some of the office work and drawings that helped to develop their practical and technical skills. Although his office records have not come to light, we do know from other sources something about two of his pupils who each received recognition as an architect in his own right and pursued very successful careers.

F. R. N. Haswell, 1834-1912, was the son of a Methodist Minister who spent most of his ministry in the north of England. Francis Robert Newton Haswell was educated at Taunton College and at the age of 15, in 1849/50, he became a pupil in the office of John Middleton where he remained until 1854. When he arrived in Darlington, he found that another pupil, Robert James Johnson, 1832-1892, was about to begin his third year with Middleton, having started in 1846. Johnson and Haswell became very good friends as well as colleagues, and on completion of his training in 1853, Johnson moved to London and spent some time in the office of George Gilbert Scott. Haswell, on completion of his training, stayed with Middleton for some time as his chief assistant and managing clerk, until he teamed up with Johnson in 1857 or thereabouts. They then spent four years together before going their separate ways in 1862.

Near the end of his apprenticeship, Haswell kept a diary which mentions Middleton, although who "JM" was and what Haswell was doing in Darlington is not made immediately obvious. It is equally frustrating not to have any of Haswell's earlier diaries if indeed any do exist. Haswell records visits he made with Johnson to medieval sites for professional training in drawing and observation, as well as for pleasure. It is likely that he and Johnson both accompanied Middleton on visits to new projects and references are certainly made to Wolsingham, Coniscliffe and Manfield. Only a mile or two from Coniscliffe and Manfield is the village of Piercebridge which was the setting for a new school with which Middleton was involved. Middleton's plans are signed and dated 1853 but subsequent correspondence shows that he did in fact delegate the supervision of this project to Haswell. The project did not go entirely to expectations and the plans had to be redrawn. All subsequent correspondence is signed by Haswell "per pro John Middleton" and provides an interesting insight into how Middleton worked with and developed those whom he had trained for the profession and how the trainee put into practice what he had learned from his mentor.

There must be many original buildings, restorations and additions by the Middleton practice in the north-east about which we may never learn. Nevertheless the time came when he decided to move on. Perhaps the poor health of his wife or his son persuaded him to seek a healthier environment; perhaps he wanted to experience at first hand the Gothic glories of the continent about which he had heard so much from colleagues, clients and acquaintances, and about which he had read so much in the popular architectural publications of his day. Whatever the reason, Middleton decided to move from Darlington although his work in the north-east did not cease entirely as we shall see later. But by 1859 at the very latest, John Middleton and his wife and son had settled in Cheltenham and in that same year he accepted the invitation to design a new church for the town.

Sources consulted:

University of Durham Library, Diocesan Records. DDR QAB/CC mortgage 37. 1851 **Coniscliffe Vicarage.**

Visit to the owners of the former Coniscliffe Vicarage in 2001.

The Builder 1850 p425. **Hartlepool, Holy Trinity Church.**

University of Durham Library, Diocesan Records, CCP A1/7 (temp) 1854-1855 Hartlepool.

Whellan, F: *Directory of Hartlepool*, 1894. Holy Trinity Church.

North, Fr. Philip: Holy Trinity, Hartlepool.

GRO, D2970 1/83 **Manfield.**

North Yorkshire County Record Office, Northallerton; PR MAN/9/1 Manfield.

Visit to the church and conversation with the incumbent of Manfield in 2001.

Listed Building Description Manfield Church. Grade II*

Milburn, Geoffrey: *Wesley Historical Society, N.E. Branch Bulletin* 53, 1990: **Haswell and Johnson.**

Potts, Graham: information about F. R. N. Haswell.

University of Durham Library Diocesan Records CCP A1/7 (temp) 1854-1855 **Pritchett and Middleton.**

Durham Record Office, County Hall: EP/RU/SN **Greatham Church** correspondence.

Listed Building Description Greatham Church Grade II*.

University of Durham Library, Diocesan Records: EP/Gre 47 (24):Greatham Church.

Durham County Record Office, County.Hall: DX 1264/1-3. **Hurworth School.**

Durham County Record Office, County Hall: D/Ed/5/3/1-2: D/Ed/5/3/3: D/Ed/5/5/30 **Piercebridge** School.

Torbay Education Services Directorate, **Torquay.**

CHAPTER V

Arrival in Cheltenham. St Mark's Church

The whereabouts of John Middleton and his family between leaving Darlington and arriving in Cheltenham have, tantalisingly, only briefly been referred to in several of the obituaries which appeared in architectural journals and the provincial press at the time of his death. Nevertheless when his son died, several published appraisals of his life and work refer to time spent with his parents travelling in Italy prior to settling in Cheltenham. Middleton would have been in his mid-thirties at the time, his wife nearing her fortieth year and their son, John Henry, aged just ten. Gothic architecture was becoming very fashionable in this country at this period and British architects were adopting much foreign detail in their churches. Middleton no doubt decided to spend some time on the continent to see and admire for himself, these glories at first hand. Unfortunately no diary of his travels has survived but what he saw obviously influenced much of his domestic and ecclesiastical work at home and his professional library in Cheltenham bore evidence of what had influenced him most.

Fig. 17 Cheltenham, St Mark

John Middleton arrived in Cheltenham early in 1859 and was joined shortly afterwards by his wife Maria and son, John Henry. By the end of the year he had purchased 13, York Terrace, one of a recently completed row of Italianate-style houses in the present St George's Road. He was soon to welcome as neighbour, the Reverend Joseph Fenn who had been appointed to the living of Christ Church and who had purchased Number 1 in the same Terrace. The two men's ages and length of service to the town were almost identical and they worked for many years to the benefit of Cheltenham, the church and education. From July to September 1860, the Middleton family was away from Cheltenham visiting Matlock and Ilkley Wells, but in August the following year, young John Henry was enrolled as a day-boy at Cheltenham College which he entered speaking fluent

Italian, no doubt acquired during the time spent on the continent with his parents. He left in December 1864 to continue his education at Exeter College, Oxford.

Middleton's obituary in *The Builder* says that "he settled in Cheltenham without the intention of practising there" but this is surprising in view of his age. To retire so young might suggest substantial private means, or perhaps ill health on his part or that of his wife or son, but in view of his vast output in the years ahead, it is unlikely that ill health was a personal consideration.

Cheltenham at this period was still under the influence of the Anglican evangelical party as personified in the Reverend Francis Close. The town was well provided with Anglican and non-conformist places of worship, but the town's population continued to expand and this brought with it the need for more seating in the Anglican churches. The population stood at about 35,000 in 1851 with new settlements being established in some of the outlying areas such as Tivoli, the Park, and St Mark's districts to name but three. This obviously created the need for more church buildings. It was not surprising therefore to learn of the proposal to build a church in what was to become the St Mark's district, and the actual wording of the announcement in *The Cheltenham Examiner* does make interesting reading:

"District Parish of St Mark, Cheltenham: a rapidly increasing population amounting to nearly 1100 souls, scattered over this wide extent of ground, has necessitated the provision of additional means of spiritual supervision and instruction. Efforts are being made with a view to erecting a church to meet the existing needs. The plans have been kindly prepared by J. Middleton Esq., a gentleman of considerable experience in Church Building, who *though for some time retired from his profession,* has generously offered to give the whole of his services as Architect as his contribution."(Author's italics)

The district referred to was part of the Parish of St Mary, Cheltenham, and comprised Lower Alstone and the north-west portion of the Gloucester Road to the limits of the parish. In 1860 the Reverend George Pruen Griffiths had been given pastoral responsibility for the area that was to become St Mark's and as there was no church or other suitable building in which to hold services, use was made of a farmhouse kitchen at the Arle extremity of the district. The area was inhabited by many poor families, mainly agricultural workers, of whom 272 were on poor rate relief and unable to make any contribution towards the cost of the new church. The Reverend Mr. Griffiths had purchased a site for £300 and in December 1861 it was conveyed to the diocese as a gift. He also advanced £500 towards the cost of building and provided £600 for the endowment. The Chairman of the Appeal Committee was Middleton's neighbour, the newly appointed Vicar of Christ Church, the Reverend Joseph Fenn and he was probably the person who had originally suggested Middleton's services. References were taken up, and it was recorded, "In reply to direct enquiries, most satisfactory testimony to Mr. Middleton's ability as an architect have (sic) been received from the Vicar of West Hartlepool, of St John the Evangelist, Darlington and from Mr. James Medland of Gloucester."

Two plans, in fact, had been submitted by Middleton before the site had been purchased and in May 1860 one of these, "for a substantial church which will seat at once 502 adults in the body, one half of the pews being given for the poor," was approved. There was also to be room for nearly one hundred children and the plans allowed for later extensions as funds became available. Advertisements inviting tenders were placed in two national journals, *The Builder* and *The Building News*, and in five Cheltenham papers and two county publications. Plans were available for inspection at St James' Infants' School in St James' Square.

Two tenders were submitted by building contractors and Mr. John Acock was successful with the lower one of £2,880. Work began on 14th June 1860 with an agreed completion date of 14th June 1861. Work progressed rapidly and at the lying of the foundation stone on 20th September 1860, tiered seats along two sides of the site enabled the one thousand persons present to watch Canon William Carus perform the ceremony He was representing the Simeon Trustees, the Patrons of the Cheltenham Rectory, in the absence of the Right Reverend Charles Baring who had just been translated from Gloucester to Durham. After the liturgical ceremonies had been performed, John Middleton presented Canon Carus with the polished oak mallet and the silver and ivory trowel, which he was invited to retain as a memento of the occasion. Middleton directed the Canon in the laying of the stone, and Mr Acock spread the mortar delicately as the stone was lowered into position, a bottle containing contemporary coins and a list of the committee members having been placed in a previously prepared cavity. By June the following year, Middleton was able to inform the committee that work was proceeding according to schedule, and that the roof was in place. A celebratory party was arranged for the workmen and their wives and Middleton served on the organising committee. The Reverend Mr. Griffiths paid one third of the cost of refreshments and those invited included the men working on the construction of the Reverend Mr. Griffiths' Parsonage house which adjoined the new church and which was to be named Hillfield.

There was a momentary drying up of funds which resulted in the postponement of the official consecration of the church as the newly appointed Bishop of Gloucester would not perform the ceremony until the church was free from debt. This eventually took place in March 1862 and Bishop William Thompson's sermon was the first to be preached in St Mark's Church. This was a happy occasion marred only by the complaints of some of the evangelical clergy present when some of their fellow clergy arrived wearing surplices rather than the more customary preaching gowns. They were informed that this was not an indication of the preference of the Bishop who, in true Anglican tradition, was happy for the clergy to "follow their own beliefs and inclinations." By the end of the following year, 1863, Bishop Thompson had been appointed Archbishop of York.

An appeal for completing the tower and spire was launched at the end of 1863 and contributors included the Reverend Joseph Fenn, the Reverend Edward Walker, Rector of Cheltenham and Major R. C. Barnard, who was soon to become a client as well as a close friend of John Middleton. By August 1864 work had started on the tower and spire as well as the boundary walls. Eighteen months later, the church's annual report announced that all was completed, "thus thoroughly finishing the building in accordance with the designs of our architect, John Middleton."

The tower was 140 feet in height and the original body of the church comprised a five bay aisled nave and a two bay chancel. The double transepts were later additions of 1889. The two tall internal arches - one to the chancel and the other to the tower - are striking features of the design. Although not rich in ornamentation, the church achieved what Middleton had been unable to accomplish in Darlington and Hartlepool and the tower and spire are visible from many parts of Cheltenham, forming a fitting memorial to Middleton's first work in his adopted town.

At the same time as the church was being built, Mr Acock was involved in building the neighbouring parsonage, Hillfield and plans were also afoot for the construction of an Infants' School for the children residing in Alstone. This additional facility would double as a lecture room for weekday services closer to the homes of the poor. The Reverend George Griffiths was licensed as Perpetual Curate of the Living on 12th November 1862 and he was occupying the parsonage by 1863. The following year, he was sharing the house, Hillfield, with his brother, Mr. E. Lloyd Griffiths, who was Middleton's solicitor. In 1865, the brother was occupying a newly erected house, The Granleys, built in the same grounds as Hillfield. Both houses are constructed in Victorian High Gothic style. Although no plans have so far come to light, both houses bear a remarkable similarity to other domestic buildings known to have been designed by Middleton, including his own home at Bayshill.

The parish needs had almost been met, but what of the plans for a school? The Reverend Mr. Griffiths had purchased a site in 1862 which was on the corner of what is today's Rowanfield Road – Alstone Lane, near the railway level crossing. He commissioned Middleton to design a school for poor persons in St Mark's district and this was opened in July 1863. It replaced the old schoolroom which had been set up by the Reverend Francis Close further up Alstone Lane towards the Gloucester Road. Middleton's school was built of red brick with the main entrance in Alstone Lane. A second school for St Mark's was built in Hatherley Lane and Middleton's drawings, dated 1876, demonstrate his eye for detail right down to to the position of every oak pin. The school opened in 1877 but like its counterpart in Alstone Lane, it has not survived, both sites now being used for housing.

Sources consulted:

After the first mention, **Gloucestershire Archives** appears as **GA.**

Dixon, Roger and Muthesius, Stefan: *Victorian Architecture.*

Personal conversations with the late Christopher Bishop.

Gloucestershire Archives, P78/8 SP1/1: SP 1/2 and P78/8 IN 1/32 **St Mark's Church.**

GA, D2970 1/169, and 3/7 and 3/9; St Mark's Church.

The Builder, 15.03.1862 and 21.02.1885

GA, P78/3 SC9: D2970/3/9: D193/207 **The schools.**

GA, P78/3 VE 21, Minutes Book of the Managers and Trustees Christ Church Schools.

Church of England Record Centre ref: 22297 pt 1; 24065 and 25485.

Listed Building Description-**The Knowle** (formerly Hillfield) SO92SW/630-1/1/353. 02/04/90.

GA, C5/6/1/1/1 Cheltenham Register of New Buildings.

GA, D4858-2/3-1907-1.**The Granleys**.

Minutes of Cheltenham Borough Council Housing Committee July 1946.

Norman's History of Cheltenham 1863.

Census Returns for Cheltenham, 1861, 1871.

Cheltenham Annuaires for the relevant years.

The Cheltenham Examiner and *The Cheltenham Looker-On* for the relevant periods.

CHAPTER VI

Middleton's Social Life in Cheltenham and the Development of the Practice

Before examining Middleton's further work in Cheltenham and beyond, it is interesting to look at how he and his family integrated into Cheltenham society, the contacts he made and his involvement in the public and civic life of the town. Their first home in the town has already been referred to above, 13, York Terrace, in today's St George's Road. In the *1861 Census* he described himself as a Landed Railway Proprietor, no doubt referring to his holdings in the Stockton and Darlington Railway. At the time of this census a young male visitor by the name of Thomas Henry Morris was staying with the family. He was aged thirteen, and had been born in Halifax. He was a contemporary of John Henry Middleton, and possibly a relation. We shall meet him again at the time of John Henry's death in 1896. The domestic staff comprised a servant and a cook, both mature ladies. Ten years later the family was living in Bayshill, in a house named Westholme, which Middleton had designed for himself, and he was then referred to as 'architect.' The son, John Henry aged twenty-four and described as an Oxford undergraduate, was also living at home. An eighteen year old niece from Derby was staying with the family and the domestic staff comprised a cook, a lady's maid and a housemaid. Twenty years later, John and Maria Middleton were still living in Westholme, and the staff had been increased to five in number, with the addition of a parlour maid and an undermaid.

At the end of 1884, Middleton sold Westholme and he and Maria moved to their third Cheltenham home, a house in St George's Road, only yards away from York Terrace and about the same distance from Westholme. This third home was named Gresham House at the time of purchase but Middleton took the name Westholme with him and this can just be seen in 2006 painted on the west front of the house. Sadly Middleton did not live long enough to fully enjoy this new home as he died within a month of moving, but Maria remained there for a further seven years before joining her son and daughter-in-law in London.

Turning to his professional life, we can safely say that John Middleton worked on his own from home, until 1868 when, perhaps realising that the amount of work he was being offered could not be done by one man alone, he decided to take on a partner. A clear and attractive indication of the beginning of the partnership appears in the first available cash book, where beautifully written in coloured, gothic script, we find,

Cash Book of Messrs Middleton and Goodman, Architects, Cheltenham. March 1st 1868.

The Articles of Partnership are signed and dated 2nd March 1868 and were deposited with Middleton's solicitor, E. Lloyd. Griffiths. Mr. A. P. Goodman paid £1050 - approaching £80,000 in today's money - for his share in the partnership for a period of ten years, and initially this entitled him to a third of all profits on any work begun after three months of the agreement, but either partner was to be entitled to undertake any gratuitous work they decided, provide the other partner was informed. Goodman was entrusted with the task of keeping the books in order and Middleton was responsible for their security. Several clauses relate to the possibility of Middleton retiring from the partnership before the completion of the ten-year period with the proviso that in such an eventuality, he would not undertake any paid commissions until Goodman's ten-year agreement had expired.

Within a short while, Middleton and Goodman had opened offices on the first floor of No 1, Bedford Buildings, a property which today makes the corner of Clarence Street and Well Walk, leading into St Mary's Churchyard. Of Mr. Goodman, little is known. The *1871 Census Return* for Cheltenham records Alfred Percy Goodman, architect, aged 30, living at Lucknow Villa, Gloucester Road, the address given for him in the partnership agreement. He was unmarried, living with his widowed mother and had been born at St Pancras, Middlesex. After 1874 his name does not appear on any extant papers relating to the practice. His address in local directories was then given as The Myrtles and he was listed under 'Resident Gentry', as was Middleton.

From 1874 until 1885 the practice was known as "Middleton and Son Architects, Cheltenham and Westminster," with 4, Storey's Gate, as the London address from 1877.

Middleton's son, John Henry, was admitted a Member of the Royal Institute of British Architects (RIBA) on 1st March 1875. He was proposed by the well-known architects, Sir George Gilbert Scott, Frederick Pepys Cockerell and his maternal uncle, James Pigott Pritchett junior, FRIBA, of Darlington. Possibly through the influence of his son, John Middleton himself applied to be admitted Fellow of the Royal Institute of British Architects in November of the same year, at a time when John Henry was on one of his adventurous travels abroad. There are few papers to do with Middleton's application in the archives of the RIBA but one is a reference in support of his application dated September 1875 and signed by the same J. P. Pritchett, FRIBA, his former partner as well as his brother-in-law. No reference was made to family or partnership connections but Pritchett stated that he had known Middleton for many years and was personally acquainted with many of his works. In addition to the known works in Cheltenham he also referred to many churches, mansions and other buildings in Yorkshire, Durham, Worcestershire, Herefordshire, Middlesex, Surrey and South Wales. Some of these will be explored later. Middleton's other sponsors were Sir George Gilbert Scott, FRIBA and Edward Middleton Barry, FRIBA. More illustrious sponsors it would be difficult to find. It was in this same year that Middleton joined Cheltenham's Freemasons' Lodge 82.

It would seem that John Henry ran the London Office until 1880 but this was in no way a formal arrangement. However a more formal partnership was entered into from January the following year with the signing of an Indenture between "John Middleton of Cheltenham, Architect, and John Henry Middleton of Cheltenham, Architect" making them co-partners in the practice. Like the partnership that had existed between Middleton and Goodman, this too was for a period of ten years but in this instance, the profits were to be shared equally from the start. John Henry was to work from the London Office, sending the accounts to his father in Cheltenham on a monthly basis. Various clauses in the Indenture refer to the possible retirement or withdrawal from the practice of either partner but the final clause makes clear that on the death of John Middleton the practice's goodwill would pass entirely to John Henry.

As had been the case in Darlington, Middleton took on several apprentices while in Cheltenham, of whom Henry Prothero was one and George Henry Phillott another. For a short while in 1864, the young and newly qualified Watson Fothergill spent several months with Middleton before moving on to Nottingham where he established his own very successful practice. Another assistant was Mr Henry Chatters who later became RIBA and left Middleton to join the Cheltenham practice of W. H. Knight. *The Cheltenham Examiner* reported at the time of Middleton's death that, "in his career he formed almost a school of architecture in the pupils who were under his tuition."

A sample of entries from the account books between 1868 and 1880 gives an interesting insight into the running expenses of the two offices:

1868	Rent to Miss Overbury, 1 quarter	£4.10.0d
	To Mary Juggins for first cleaning of office and five weeks' attendance	16.0d
	To Mr Alibru(?) for moving office furniture	17.2d
1869	Prints of All Saints	15.0d
	Painting office	£1.06.0d
1870	Paid Mitchell 1 week's salary	£1.10.0d
	Subscription to architectural exhibition	10.3d

A long list then follows of expenses for office furniture and supplies.

1871	Christmas tip to postman	2.0d
1873	Rent now	£7.00.0d
	Coins for Tivoli Church	3.9d
1874	Marshall for picking lock	1.0d
	Marshall for mending door	2.0d
1877	Rent and housekeeper, Storey's Gate	£10.0.2d
	Painting name at Storey's Gate	12.0d
1878	Parcel to Sowerby	2.6d
1879	Rent Storey's Gate	£6.14.6d
	Copy of Godings Cheltenham	6.0d
1880	Rent Storey's Gate	£8.08.0d

Thereafter, such recording ceases and expenses are listed on a page for each client and include postage, plans, travel, telegrams and prints of proposed designs. Between 1868 and 1874 travel expenses are listed frequently for 'Mr. M' and, less frequently, for 'Mr. G.'

L. W. Barnard, FRIBA, writing in 1948 recalled life in the Middleton office at the time of John Middleton's death in 1885. He described conditions that were undoubtedly as true at the time of Middleton and Goodman as they were in the mid 1880s.

"Drawings had to be prepared with not half the mechanical aids we have now.... .We had to rub ink from a stick which if you were doing much ink drawing had to be done two or three times a day. Added to this we had not got then of course any advantage such as telephones or means of transport. Even a bicycle was not used at the office before 1890.....and assistants had to get to the work by walking..... The work was better then especially as regards joinery. John Middleton himself was very fond of stop chamfers and square joints with mortices and tenons often designed by himself. As regards planning, the planning of a church designed by John Middleton 90 years ago is as good as any we can do now (1948)."

Barnard also remembered Middleton quite clearly in a more intimate role.

"As a small boy I knew him more or less as he was a great friend of my father (Major R. C. Barnard) and when John Henry grew up, I might say he was an even greater friend of my father. He was also godfather to my brother Sedgwick".

Middleton was fortunate in having skilled craftsmen to execute his designs. As local firms such as Messrs Boulton, Letheren, Martyn and Emms and others, feature so prominently in his commissions, a peep into their backgrounds would seem appropriate. Richard Lockwood Boulton and his two brothers started the firm of Boulton and Swales in London c1838. They soon had branches in Birmingham and Worcester. On the death of his two elder brothers R. L Boulton moved to Cheltenham around 1866-1867. It may well be that the opportunities presented in the demand for church building and restoration, and the presence of an architect such as Middleton, who specialised in such contracts, influenced Boulton's decision to move. He had been an exhibitor at the Royal Academy, had been awarded medals for his sculpture both in Paris and London's Great Exhibition of 1851, and had carried out work for eminent architects such as Scott, Pugin, Street and Bodley. The firm became the country's leading ecclesiastical sculptors bringing to life the designs of many of the great Victorian architects including those mentioned above.

William Letheren by contrast was one of the earlier metalwork craftsmen in Cheltenham. He established his Vulcan Iron Works at Lansdown, near the town's Midland Station in the 1860s. His Art Manufactory soon became well known internationally and he received commissions from places as far apart as Florence, Bombay and Shanghai. Middleton's Ledgers make frequent references to work contracted to him.

H. H. Martyn was born in 1842 in Worcester and at the age of 19, he began his career as an architectural carver attending evening classes at art school in the town. He then worked for R. L. Boulton and moved with him when he came to Cheltenham. In 1874 he went into partnership with another Boulton employee, a wood carver, Mr. E. A. Emms. Their partnership lasted for fourteen years, until 1888 when Martyn formed his own company with the object of "producing the best in wood, stone and marble carving, wrought iron, decorative plasterwork, stained glass, cast bronze, modelling, sculpture, furniture and cabinet making." Another former apprentice of Boulton, was the sculptor A. B. Wall who was working in the Prestbury Road by the 1870s.

Within two years of arriving in Cheltenham the Reverend Joseph Fenn nominated John Middleton to serve as Vicar's Warden for Christ Church. In very neat copper plate writing, Middleton signed his acceptance, a procedure which was to continue annually right up to 1878 when he and his co-Warden, Major General McCausland, asked to be relieved of their duties. In addition to serving as Churchwarden, Middleton also served as secretary to Christ Church School from 1863-1875 and he kept meticulous records of events during this period. One entry in particular for March 1868 shows his personal involvement in the day to day happenings at the school: "The Reverend and Mrs Hopkins and Mr Middleton, accompanied by a Police detective, visited the school to examine and enquire about some money stolen from a school drawer."

From 1863 to 1874 John Middleton was also secretary to the Cheltenham School of Art and in 1863 he was a founder member of the Cheltenham Permanent Library, later becoming its first treasurer and a member of the Council. It was publicly acknowledged that it was due to his enthusiasm more than any other that the Library had been founded. Through this connection he met future clients many of whom became family friends, including the Reverend Alfred Barry, Principal of Cheltenham College; the Reverend T. A. Southwood of Cheltenham College; the Reverend Dr Morton Brown, Minister of the Congregational Church and Major R. C. Barnard who was to become one of his closest personal friends. In 1870 Middleton became an Ordinary Elected Member of Council of Cheltenham Ladies' College which brought him into contact with Dr. E. T. Wilson father of the future Antarctic explorer, and Mrs James Owen, "that friend of Dorothea Beale who with Mrs Middleton became intimates of Miss Beale from about 1880." In 1876 Middleton was a Founder Member of the Bristol and Gloucestershire Archaeological Society and carried out the role of secretary to the Cheltenham Branch of that Society until his death in 1885. However his main public service contribution to Cheltenham was in his capacity as one of the Improvement Commissioners for the Middle Ward of the town, a position he filled from 1863 to 1875. To qualify as a Commissioner one had to own property to the value of at least £1000 and to reside within five miles of the centre of Cheltenham. In his time as Commissioner, Middleton served on the Sewerage and Drainage Committee, the Public Cemetery Committee and the Water Supply Committee.

Politically, Middleton was a Conservative and his name was given some prominence in the election broadsheets, as a supporter of Charles Schreiber who was standing against the serving Liberal, Colonel Berkeley. On this occasion Schreiber was returned victorious. Middleton's political persuasion was again in the public domain in 1871 when he supported a local candidate for election as a Commissioner for the East Ward in the town. There had been some dispute as to whether the candidate's political views were too liberal, but Middleton publicly vouched for the candidate's commitment to the Conservative agenda and he was elected. The pro-Liberal *Cheltenham Examiner* in acknowledging the appointment assured its readers, "We treat any assertion vouched for by Mr. Middleton with the greatest respect."

From about 1874 Middleton became less involved with public office although he continued actively to support organisations in which he had a particular interest. One of these was 'Friends in Council' of which he was a member for seventeen years. The organisation was an informal club for like-minded professionals who met to discuss and debate matters of social and literary interest. It had been founded in 1862 by Major R. C. Barnard with a limit of twelve elected members. The club owed its origin to a similar venture at Cambridge - The Apostles - the aim of which was to provide intellectual entertainment for professional people. Friends in Council met in the homes of members, the host being appointed President for the evening. A paper was presented on a previously advertised topic - politics and religion were barred - and refreshments were provided. Most members were from the clerical, teaching or military professions, the majority with Oxford or Cambridge degrees. Guests could be invited and Dorothea Beale was present on several occasions. Middleton was elected in 1868 and he presided at a meeting each year from 1869 to 1884 with one exception. Topics which he presented ranged from "Dennis' Cities of Etruria" to "Darwin's Descent of Man," from "Assyrian Discoveries" to "The Talmud" and "Habitations of Man in All Ages." Most of the members were people for whom he worked professionally or with whom he served on committees.

It has already been noted that Middleton was a Freemason and in this capacity he contributed to the fabric of St Mary's Church, Cheltenham's ancient parish church. The church was restored during the late 1870s and the Cheltenham Lodge of Freemasons suggested that they might do something towards its embellishment. They offered to fill in the east window with coloured glass and this offer was accepted. The project was placed in the hands of a small committee one of whose members was John Middleton. He had been initiated into Foundation Lodge 82 at Cheltenham Masonic Hall in December 1876, the year in which he became FRIBA. The window was handed over at the close of a special Wednesday afternoon service on 26th May 1880 and carried the acknowledgement "To the Glory of God this window is erected by the Freemasons of Cheltenham AD 1880." *The Cheltenham Examiner* reported the occasion and described the procession into the church of clergy and the eight Freemasons of the committee. Middleton is named and like his colleagues, he was attired "in the varied clothing of their several ranks in the Craft, from the rich purple and gold of the Grand Provincial Lodge to the pale blue and silver of the ordinary Lodges, and with jewels whose significance is not for the uninitiate to enquire." Thus ended Middleton's contribution to the fabric of the Parish Church although in 1880 he presented the font as a gift to the daughter church of St Matthew just across the way in Clarence Street.

From a domestic perspective, little is known about Middleton's family life. Obviously money was not a problem and the Middletons enjoyed the comforts of a personally designed home on Bayshill. Perhaps understandably for the period, Maria Middleton does not feature prominently in her husband's professional or civic life but this may also be due to the medical condition of their son, John Henry. He was not a healthy youth and had been forced to withdraw from his university studies on health grounds which we shall explore later. This meant that his five or six years back in Cheltenham, in which most of the time he confined himself to his room, placed a considerable burden on his parents. The Dowager Countess Dunraven visited the Middletons at their home in June 1867 and she wrote in her diary, that Mrs Middleton was in deep distress at the dangerous, indeed hopelessness (sic) of her only son and child but that she seemed better in herself. A year later, December 1868, after another visit, the Countess recorded how sad it was to find both Mrs Middleton and John Henry lying on their beds with incurable (diseases?). She also wrote of her sympathy for Middleton himself, in that his wife and child seemed to have little hope of enjoying the comforts and affections provided for them by "dear Mr Middleton," although he seemed to be wonderfully resigned to the situation.

Nevertheless John Henry did not waste these days of confinement and on good days he read and studied avidly which helped to prepare him for the distinguished, albeit short career which lay ahead.

Sources consulted:

GA, D2970 2/2 First Cash Book, **Middleton and Goodman**.

GA, D2216 box 25 pt 2. Articles of Partnership 1868.

RIBA Archives, the Middleton File and Nomination Papers Vol 5 1873-1879.

Norman, George, *The Provincial Grand Lodge of Gloucestershire.* 1911.

GA, D2216 box 25 pt 2. Articles of Partnership 1881.

Brand, Ken: *Watson Fothergill Architect*, for Nottingham Civic Society 1997.

Barnard, L. W, *Ninety Years Past.* 1949.

Boulton: Biographical notes supplied by the late Cheltenham firm of Bryant and Coates.

Whitaker, John: *The Best.* ***H.H. Martyn*** *and Co.*,1998.

Christ Church School Log Book 1864-1872, information provided by Jill Waller.

Various *Annuaires & Directories for Cheltenham 1863-1880.*

Transactions of the Bristol and Gloucestershire Archaeological Society Vol X 1973.

Cheltenham Reference Library, Local Studies Department, 63G637. '**History of Friends in Council.**'

Public Record Office, Northern Ireland, Belfast. **The Dunraven Diaries. (Ref Chapter XII)**

Correspondence and conversations with the late Christopher Bishop, MA, RIBA.

CHAPTER VII

Further Cheltenham Churches

During his time in Cheltenham, Middleton built up an extensive practice and has justifiably been credited with being one of the most accomplished local architects of the mid-nineteenth century. In his church work, for which he is best known, he came down firmly in support of the ecclesiological movement begun in 1839 with the Cambridge Camden Society. The Society's influence through its journal, *The Ecclesiologist* which first appeared in 1841, is evident in most of his church work. Galleries and high box-pews were dismantled, and churches were designed or reordered to emphasise the sacrament rather than the sermon. This was symbolised in the emphasis placed on the altar rather than on the pulpit and the style of architecture reflected the past in the use of the English Decorated style of the early fourteenth century. Fashions had changed and Cheltenham needed to move away from that non-conformist influence which still flourished in the town when Middleton arrived there. The five new Victorian churches he designed illustrate his attempt to restore that medieval style of church architecture which placed an emphasis on the chancel and the sanctuary. Each church also had a clearly defined nave, aisles, baptistry and porch. The chancel was raised above the level of the nave and approached through a recognisable arch. The stalls for the clergy faced north and south and were placed just inside the chancel. The sanctuary too was raised so that it was higher than the chancel and clearly separated from it with an altar rail. If finances allowed a tower and spire were also included in the plan. This became Middleton's goal and one which sadly he was only able to realise fully at St Mark's and Clearwell in the Forest of Dean. He did however develop a personal style for the exterior of his churches, preferring a strong masculine appearance, with contrasting stone textures and a love for rusticated stone. However this external appearance often does not do justice to the beauty of the interiors with their polychrome decoration and ornate carved detail. This is especially true for Holy Apostles and All Saints, Cheltenham.

The building of St Mark's, Cheltenham, has already been described, but in the 1860s two further churches were commenced in the town and these were joined by two more during the 1870s. Addressing these in the order in which the foundation stones were laid leads us first to All Saints Church. This is the church which the architectural historian Goodhart-Rendel described as "a splendid example of what Gilbert Scott was always aiming at but never achieved - complete Gothic self assurance with Victorian punch." The church is unique in Middleton's portfolio in that it was designed with a high church congregation in mind and its internal decoration and ordering reflect this.

Fig. 18 Cheltenham, All Saints

The events which led to the building of All Saints were long and protracted but essentially revolved around a difference in tradition between the evangelical Patrons of St John's Church in the town and its Priest-in-Charge the Reverend George Roberts, who sympathised with the more Catholic tradition. In February 1864, *The Cheltenham Examiner* carried a notice for "the proposed erection of a new church by the congregation of St John's and their friends." Subscriptions were invited from sympathisers towards the building and endowment of the new church where the promoters could enjoy that freedom of worship and of doctrinal teaching which had been their privilege for the past eleven years at St John's.

A building committee was formed and by 1865 a distinct ecclesiastical district had been mapped out. The recently appointed bishop of the diocese, Bishop Charles Ellicott gave his approval to the initiative and allowed five years for completion of the church. John Middleton was asked to draw plans and *The Builder* of 18th November that year announced that the site was soon to be enclosed and work on the church could begin. Just five weeks after this announcement, Dr. Ellicott laid the foundation stone, "the weather for the time of year being exceedingly fine." This was the bishop's first such ceremony since being appointed to the diocese. From the start, the promoters of the new church made it clear that All Saints was to be a house of daily prayer, with the Morning and Evening Offices, weekly Communion, and the observance of Fasts and Festivals. Mr. Roberts was nominated the first incumbent by the promoters but thereafter the Bishop would have the right of presentation and the stipend would come from voluntary contributions.

There was an impressive gathering for the laying of the foundation stone, again with some clergy wearing gowns, and others in surplices. Middleton assisted the Bishop

Fig. 19 Cheltenham, All Saints

in the laying of the stone and presented him with the trowel and mallet. Three months later the plans were on view for anyone who wished to make a contribution towards the costs of the church and by November 1866 the church was already about fourteen feet above ground. Sadly, it appears that the Reverend Mr. Roberts had invested too much of his own money in the project and his subsequent bankruptcy meant that under Canon Law he could not continue his ministry. A successor was appointed and pending completion some of the church services were held in a meeting hall in the High Street.

All Saints Church was consecrated on 2nd November 1868 and the Early French Gothic style with the extremely rich interior were much admired by all present. In one respect, All Saints is typical of Middleton's work in that he used contrasting stone texture to add to the external appearance, in this case, Cleeve Hill stone with Bath stone dressings. *The Cheltenham Examiner* gave a very detailed description of the church and heaped praise upon Middleton: "The style....while giving a grand simplicity of outline, admits of great artistic treatment, of which circumstances Mr Middleton has fully availed himself....Credit should be given to Mr Middleton for the taste he has shown in the design and superintendence of the minutest detail." The Dowager Countess Dunraven visited Middleton at his home later in the year and together they visited All Saints. The Countess recorded how very much she admired the building.

The church was by no means complete at this stage, however, and internal adornment was achieved gradually. It was not until the following year, 1869, that the local press could report that the church had lost its unfinished appearance and was " now a thing of real beauty." This beauty was most noticeable in the roofing in the nave and transepts, where the naked timbers had been panelled, and in the chancel where richly moulded and groined arches had been introduced. In the sanctuary itself, the roof panels were not filled in but painted and the colour gave a rich glow to the work. Three new windows were added shortly after the consecration which together with the stone carving and marble decoration added a certain feeling of opulence to the building. Minton tiles of a costly and appropriate pattern and colour had been used in the chancel while the sanctuary steps and risers were of green and red serpentine marble. New brass gas standards and an ornate brass altar rail had been provided and the altar, of oak with panelled front and ends enriched with ebony shafts and inlay had been made to Middleton's design.

Middleton continued to be involved with All Saints for many years, and must have been delighted with the challenge of ongoing additions to this, his most artistic masterpiece. In response to unfavourable remarks about the original pulpit, he designed a new one which was carved by local sculptor R. L. Boulton in 1872 and this was installed at the same time as the reredos which Middleton had also designed. A detailed description of the sanctuary and reredos was given in *The Builder* and is worth repeating:

> "The reredos runs round the East end of the chancel and is divided into five compartments, each one containing three arches. The divisions are marked by angels two feet six inches high, standing under canopies above which rise marble pillars which are carried up to support the groining of the chancel. Of these angels, some are holding symbols of the Passion while others have their hands joined in an attitude of prayer. Smaller angels playing musical instruments occupy the spandrels. The plinth pillars are of English, Irish and Italian marble, the larger angels of Caen stone and the rest of the work is alabaster. The three centre compartments forming the reredos proper contain representations in relief of Our Lord bearing his cross, the Crucifixion and the Entombment. The other arches are filled with incised work of black cement on an alabaster ground. At the north side is the Bishop's Throne with a crocheted canopy and on the south side is the credence and a three seat sedilia."

In 1909 alterations were made to the reredos proper by the architect Temple Moore. This included altering the style of the arches from pointed to trefoil and raising it considerably so that it became more visible from the nave. The arched canopy above the altar is also by Temple Moore.

The boundary walls, gates and railings were all part of Middleton's design and his final contribution was the vestry completed in 1883. Various additions have been made since Middleton's day, notably the west doorway with carved tympanum by A. B. Wall, c1885, but there have been few alterations. One proposed addition while he was working on All Saints was for a chancel screen. His son, John Henry prepared a design for an oak screen in 1879 and a facsimile was erected in the church over the Christmas period to test the reaction of the congregation. It met with little enthusiasm and nothing was done until 1894 when the present screen was installed to the design of Henry Prothero.

All Saints was built and remains today, a fine example of a church intended for the celebration of High Church liturgy. Middleton put every morsel of his artistic, architectural and ecclesiological skill into what must have been his most challenging and successful commission both in its structural design and in its opulent fittings.

While work was still in progress on All Saints, Middleton had designed another church for the town for which the foundation stone had already been laid. This church at Charlton Kings, intended to be dedicated to The Twelve Apostles, was eventually named Holy Apostles and was the realisation of an individual's dream. Charles Cooke Higgs was a wealthy land and property owner who lived at Langton House on the London Road. St Mary's was the Parish Church of Charlton Kings but it was situated in the middle of the village, some distance from where Higgs lived. In view of the steady increase in the number of 'better class residents' in his part of Charlton Kings, Higgs took it upon himself to donate a site for a new, additional church together with £1000 towards building costs. The site donated was a triangular plot at the junction of the London and Cirencester roads, adjacent to that on which his own house stood. His appeal to residents for subscriptions towards the new church did not result in an enthusiastic response but he was determined to proceed and engaged John Middleton to draw the plans. Higgs' approach to the Ecclesiastical Commissioners for a grant met with a blank refusal so he decided to finance the whole project from his own pocket.

The Cheltenham Examiner reported the start of work on the new church in September 1865 and advised its readers that "Mr. Middleton's plans indicate that the church will be one of the handsomest specimens of modern architecture in the county." The shape of the site had presented problems but this had been admirably addressed by the architect and as the west end would be the most noticeable feature as one left Cheltenham, much artistic design had been put into this elevation. It was also reported that

Fig. 20 Cheltenham, Holy Apostles

once the tower was completed "further comfort can be taken from the fact that the new church will look down on St Gregory's," the new Catholic Church, with its two hundred feet spire.

Nine months before St Mark's had been completed, the foundation stone of Holy Apostles Church was laid by Mr. Higgs himself. The actual service was conducted by the Vicar of the Parish of Charlton Kings who delivered "a few remarks suitable to the occasion," perhaps indicating by his brevity that he was not entirely in favour of the project. Just sixteen months later the church was well on the way to completion. The date for the opening could not be finalised due in part to Mr Higgs' dispute with the diocese over who had the right to nominate the incumbent and it was in fact five years after the laying of the foundation stone and two years after completion, that the opening eventually took place. A large congregation was present for the service on Monday 5th June 1871 which was conducted by Bishop Ellicott. Local press reports of the occasion pay tribute to the taste and professional ability of Middleton and focus on the colourful roof in the sanctuary, the pulpit, the Caen stone reredos with its alabaster and marble ornamentation and the oak seating. *The Cheltenham Examiner* gave the fullest account of the opening of which the following is a summary.

'A visitor must be struck with the lightness and elegance of the whole building. The stem like pillars of the nave supporting the symmetrical perpendicular arches are enriched with chastely chiselled capitals ... of leaves, fruit, flowers and birds. The eye is charmed with the profusion and excellence of the sculpture ...in the nave... or the aisles... or in the chancel where the sculptor and decorator have vied with each other in producing rich and varied effects; where the walls are encrusted with groups of angels in various positions of worship or adoration and where the roof is a burnished vault glowing with gold and pigment of various colours... The reredos is a triumph of the chisel. The material, marble of two or three colours, is wrought into simple but exquisitely harmonious patterns and the recess is appropriately filled with a representation of the Last Supper...A survey of the whole building leads us irresistibly to the conclusion that a lavish and or at the same time, a discriminating bounty has been exercised in the erection of a place of worship which is, all circumstances considered, quite unique in the county.'

Fig. 21 Cheltenham, Holy Apostles

The stone carving was by R. L. Boulton and the ironwork by Mr Letheren.

The consecration of the church was not performed until 1885, after Higgs' death. Although the tower and spire were never completed, Holy Apostles is one of Middleton's gems. In 1970 a fire gutted the church and the sanctuary ceiling was destroyed. The present ceiling is a replica of the original. The nave ceiling also had to be replaced and this was done at a lower level than the original. Thankfully nearly all of the nave pews were saved from destruction. Holy Apostles is the only one of Middleton's churches in which his name is to be seen 'set in stone' - carved on a riser at floor level behind the pulpit, "John Middleton, Architect."

As well as donating the site and in the event, paying for the building of Holy Apostles Church, C. C. Higgs felt passionately that here was a need for a school for the children of the immediate neighbourhood. He gave a site next to the church together with £1000 for the provision of a boys' school capable of accommodating two hundred pupils. Several plans and drawings were signed Middleton and Goodman 1872 and show provision for a teacher's house as well as the school. The foundation stone was laid by Mr. Higgs on 1st August 1872 in the presence of one hundred neighbouring gentry and in the evening a celebratory supper was held for the twenty or so workmen at the London Inn. Toasts were proposed to the architects, Middleton and Goodman and to Mr. Hawkins the builder.

The school was formally opened one year later and it was revealed that the final cost had amounted to £2000. Celebrations began with a service in the new church, at the end of which a procession made its way to the new schoolrooms. A second but much briefer ceremony followed after which Mr. Higgs declared the school open. The original intention to educate boys only was altered to include children of both genders. *The Cheltenham Examiner* again provided a full description of the building which was intended to promote the principles of the National Society, and which would have the status of a Voluntary Church of England school.

As one can see today, the building is in the Middle Pointed style of architecture with an apsidal west end facing towards Cheltenham. Internally there were three classrooms and the roofs were of open timber slightly stained and relieved with coloured stencilling. In the room which makes the apsidal west end, there was a very complicated roof structure and in one of the other rooms, there was a panelled wall frieze below the wall plate. The carved interior corbels seem rather grand for what was a small parish school, but the whole structure was an appropriate complement to the neighbouring church. There is a western bell turret and the roof is capped with decorative ridge tiles. In 2002-2003 the school was converted into two dwellings but fortunately most of the external features have been retained.

Mr. Higgs completed his gifts to the parish with the provision of a handsome drinking fountain at the road junction just below the school. Its erection is recorded in the report of the opening of the school but Middleton's drawings for it have not come to light. The fountain provided a suitable adornment for such a prominent site but today is desperately in need of some preservation work to combat the effects of pollution caused by heavy traffic.

The fourth of Middleton's parish churches to be completed was that of St Philip and St James in Leckhampton. The neighbouring St Stephen's Church had been started

Fig. 22 Cheltenham, Ss Philip & James

in 1873 but was still a mission church within the Christ Church Parish. The original St Philip's Church, Leckhampton had been consecrated in 1840 and was "badly built, badly ventilated and inconveniently arranged." It was a typical 'preaching box' with an abundance of galleries and a tower at the east end. It had been built for the people who inhabited this poorer area of Leckhampton, but by the 1870s it was totally unsuited to the more affluent population which was moving into the area. Various proposals were discussed as to how to address the problem of the shortage of seating. The building of a new church was considered on a new site, but this was rejected. Eventually it was decided to erect a new and larger church on the existing site, in such a manner that ordinary services would be interrupted as little as possible during building work. John Middleton was consulted and in February 1879 he was informed that his plans and specifications had been accepted as long as they did not exceed the £2000 so far raised by appeal. When Middleton produced the tenders he had received, the lowest was accepted, even though it was £300 above the available funds, which by that time stood at £2520. A faculty was granted on May 29th and work began immediately. By the end of the first week of June a temporary east wall had been constructed within the church and the demolition of the tower and walls at the east end of the building had begun. The congregation continued to worship in the remaining part of the church until the new chancel and transepts were completed beyond the temporary east wall.

The foundation stone was laid in September 1879 by the Vicar of the Parish but it was only at this point that consideration was given as to where the congregation might worship when the rest of the church was demolished. Middleton suggested that the existing nave should be demolished at once, new foundations laid and the external walls built to a height of three or four feet. Within this shell, a temporary iron church could be erected for worship, while the permanent church was built around it. The whole process would take no more than two months. This was agreed and the iron church was erected as proposed. Not once did building work interrupt a Sunday service and only rarely a weekday one. Praise was lavished upon Middleton: "The work adds, if that were possible, to the high reputation of the architect... a gent to whom Cheltenham is indebted for several of its most ornamental and characteristic public buildings." It was not all plain sailing, however, and there were problems with the building committee as well as neighbours whose homes stood alongside the new north transept.

Fig. 23 Cheltenham, Ss Philip & James

The committee was not in favour of his choice of glass for the chancel windows and neighbours threatened legal action because their property was being adversely affected by the building activity immediately next to it. An out of court settlement was eventually agreed.

In Easter week 1882, Bishop Ellicott consecrated the new church of Ss Philip and James, Leckhampton. The act of consecration was set within the context of Holy Communion and the Bishop constantly referred to "this noble and spacious house of prayer and praise." In more secular vein, *The Cheltenham Looker-On* reported,

> "The structure may well be pronounced a marvel of mechanical skill and ingenuity and as an example of ecclesiastical architecture it may challenge comparison inside or out with any of its type."

Fig. 24 Cheltenham, Ss Philip and James. The Middleton Memorial Window

At the reception which followed, Middleton was once more subjected to lavish praise from all sides: "You can tell the chastened and beautiful task which he accomplishes in his work wherever he goes and I hope you will rise with me and offer tribute to the accomplished gentleman who has enabled you to erect this church so beautifully," was the Archdeacon of Gloucester's tribute, one of many. Middleton did find courage to reply to these compliments and in so doing he acknowledged the great distinction it was for him, "to have the work approved by men of such refined taste, as it affords me full compensation for the labour and care necessary for the building."

The church was constructed in the Early English style, and the interior was impressive with a nave roof of wooden panels supported by shafts resting on moulded corbels. The nave arches were supported on Mansfield stone pillars with moulded caps and bases. The clerestory above was quite impressive and the aisles were lit by two-light windows. At the west end Middleton incorporated a large circular window from the original church, beneath which was a handsome external door. The chancel was approached through a lofty gothic arch supported on either side on black marble shafts. The roof timbers of the chancel were supported on similar marble shafts with richly carved corbels. The chancel was separated from the transepts by richly moulded arches and polychromatic stonework. The east window was of five lights. The pulpit and font were carved by Martyn and Emms of Cheltenham The present reredos is an addition of 1889 and the chancel screen dates from 1902.

In April 1888 a stained window was placed in the north aisle in memory of John Middleton. It is the work of his son, John Henry and was presented by the family as Ss Philip and James was one of the last commissions on which he had been engaged prior to his death. *The Cheltenham Examiner* described it as a most appropriate tribute, "which will preserve from oblivion for many generations to come, the name of a gentleman who was ever ready to assist in the promotion of any good work in which his professional skill might be of service."

The church was planned with a tower and spire but as with most of Middleton's churches funding for the spire was not forthcoming. The copper saddleback steeple and fleche were provided in 1903 to the design of Middleton's successors in the practice.

It is puzzling that in the speeches made after the consecration of Ss Philip and James, no reference was made to St Stephen's, a church only some half a mile distant. St Stephen's Church was built in two distinct phases and qualifies as the last of Middleton's Cheltenham churches to be completed.

Christ Church had been consecrated in 1840 and the district it served extended as far as the Park, where it shared a boundary with Leckhampton parish. Many of those who attended Christ Church were unaware of the poverty and poor housing conditions that characterised the rapidly expanding and densely populated district of Tivoli which lay to the south-east of their parish. Soon after his arrival in the town, Middleton's contemporary, the Reverend Joseph Fenn was desperate to do something to address the situation. As Vicar of the district in which this poverty existed he saw the need to provide church accommodation for these people and he eventually persuaded his flock to support the building of a "Mission Church for these deserving poor." Eventually in 1873 a site was purchased and within six months work had begun on the building of the church, "of similar description and not inferior to St Mark's." Plans were prepared by Middleton for what is in fact the present chancel of St Stephen's, with provision for enlargement at a later date if this proved desirable.

Fig. 25 Cheltenham, St Stephen

By the time the foundation stone was laid on 4th November 1873 by Bishop Ellicott, the walls were several feet above ground. In the cavity beneath the stone, Middleton placed the box containing contemporary coins (entered in his cash book referred to in chapter VI) and a vellum list of subscribers. Just one year later, 30th October 1874, the formal opening of St Stephen's Church took place. In his address Dr. Ellicott emphasised that the church was to be a free, open church providing for the poor of the district amongst whom the Vicar's wife had worked so tirelessly. He also hinted that the architect's design for a full completion of the church would not be long in coming to fruition.

Fig. 26 Cheltenham, St Stephen

The press reports of the opening described the different coloured stone which Middleton had employed and the arches which were to eventually form the entrance into the north and south transepts. It must be remembered too, that the present open chancel arch was at that time, a bricked-in temporary and exterior west wall, pending the anticipated extension of the church. The east wall contained the original large four light window with a rich arch mould springing from marble columns. The south wall contained three windows, one in the sanctuary and two between the present pillars. The north wall contained only one window in the sanctuary. The roof is as it was when constructed and its open timbers with moulded cornices deserve closer examination as do the marble columns and richly carved corbels.

Just seven years later, on December 19th 1881, it was decided to proceed with the completion of the church to Middleton's design. Exactly two years after this decision was taken, Bishop Ellicott was again at St Stephen's for the consecration of the church which at first he called handsome, "but on second thoughts, a beautiful church. The chasteness of the architecture, the delicate carving, the proportions, are all calculated to awaken feelings of admiration."

The building which Bishop Ellicott consecrated is the smallest of Middleton's Cheltenham churches and, after St Mark's, the plainest, although the lack of ornamentation is relieved by the introduction of blue Forest and red Mansfield stone. The nave roof was of a very high pitch and perfectly semi-circular, of panelled woodwork and moulded ribs, with carved bosses at the intersections. The nave consisted of six bays with clerestory above. The west wall was ornamented with an arcade of small arches running across the width of the nave.

The mission church now became the chancel and sanctuary of the Church of St Stephen, Tivoli, and the planned reredos was installed in time for the consecration. This intricate carving now adorns the lower part of the west wall. The altar and pulpit are to Middleton's design, the former closely resembling that at All Saints and the pulpit replacing an earlier temporary one. Mr. R. L. Boulton was responsible for the stone carving in the chancel but Martyn and Emms completed the work in the nave and aisles. The screen is a later addition of 1897.

Yet again a tower and spire were planned for the church but were never completed and the north and south porches were added shortly after Middleton's death. Although St Stephen's has a dull and uninteresting exterior, David Verey was quite right in saying, "It has a successful and carefully detailed interior of richest decoration about which there is a feeling of completeness of design."

Within the space of twenty-three years, John Middleton had created five new churches in one town - no mean feat. Although added to or reordered by succeeding generations, they still stand as proud witnesses to the Christian faith and as memorials to the architect who adopted Cheltenham as his home.

Sources consulted:

GA, P78/2, D2970 1/28. **All Saints' Church.**

GA, Diocesan Records F1/1/1877/2.

Church of England Record Centre, Ref.31713-All Saints Church.

All Saints Log Book kindly provided by the Churchwarden.

Amber, Lillian: *All Saints Church, A Short Guide*, c1980.

Gloucester Journal, 10 August 1884. **Holy Apostles Church.**

Church of England Record Centre, Holy Apostles Church, Ref 42135

Paget, Mary, *A History of Charlton Kings*, 1989.
GA, D2970 1/26, Holy Apostles Church.
GA, D2970 1/27 **Holy Apostles School**.
GA, Diocesan Archives F3/6 10/130/2 Holy Apostles Church and School.
Charlton Kings Local History Society *Journal* No 26.
The Church at the Crossroads- *A Holy Apostles Millennium Celebration 2000.*
GA, P198/2, **Ss Philip and James Church.**
Church of England Record Centre Ss Philip and James Church, Ref 12349 & 27472.
Gloucestershire Notes and Queries, Vol III pp 96-97.
GA, D2970 3/9 No 53 and 107. Ss Philip and James.
GA, D2970/180 Ss Philip and James.
Cheltenham Chronicle and Gloucestershire Graphic 22 November 1902.
GA, D2970 3/9 and 2970/229 **St Stephen's Church**.
Church of England Record Centre, St Stephen's Church Ref 48000.
Kirby, I, and Torode, B, *St Stephen's Church History* 1973.
St Stephen's Church Archives held at the church.
GA, D843/4/1 p356 St Stephen's Chancel.
Blake, Steven, *Cheltenham's Churches and Chapels.* 1979.
Scotland, Nigel, (ed), *A Gloucestershire Gallery* 1993. Chapter 15 by Hugh Greenhalf.

CHAPTER VIII

Restorations and Rebuilding

Although Middleton is best remembered in Cheltenham for the five new churches he designed, there were many other demands made on his professional skills in the area at the same time. As early as 1866 he was negotiating the rebuilding of St Peter's Church in Leckhampton; in 1868 he was completing similar work at Coberley and as late as 1876 he was supervising the enlargement and refurbishment of St Mary's Parish Church in Charlton Kings. In addition to these major undertakings he was also involved with many other smaller commissions ranging from more minor church work to the building of private houses, schools and hospitals.

Middleton's professional reputation had been confirmed with the building of St Mark's Church. Added to this, his son's avid interest in archaeology, antiquities and art, ensured that the practice, from its earliest days, was resourced with more than adequate expertise to undertake the most challenging restorations, although the actual methods employed by Middleton were not always above criticism. This is especially true when one looks at his work at Coberley and Charlton Kings.

Fig. 27 Leckhampton, St Peter

One of his earliest attempts at the restoration of a medieval church in Gloucestershire amounted almost to a total rebuilding. This was at Leckhampton, just south of Cheltenham. The fourteenth century church comprised a nave, a south aisle of three bays, a chancel east of the tower with its slender spire, and a priest's door in the north wall of the chancel. There was a porch in the centre of the north wall of the nave and inside, all the walls were plastered and whitewashed. Seating was available for approximately four hundred and fifty persons which was totally inadequate for the population of the village which had increased noticeably during the mid 1800s. In May 1864 the Vestry decided to seek professional advice on the advantages to be gained from necessary repairs to the north and west walls as opposed to removing and rebuilding them and enlarging the building. Middleton was consulted, and his drastic plans for the enlargement as well as the restoration of the church were accepted. By the end of 1864, the church had been almost totally demolished and only the chancel, tower and spire were left intact. Appeals had been launched, grants applied for, and by 1867, the vestry was able to report that the work of rebuilding was in a forward state, but they were still a long way from completion due to a lack of funds.

Work continued as further funds became available and although Middleton's work left little evidence of the original church he did address the issues raised in the faculty application. The south aisle wall was partially rebuilt, and a new north aisle was provided to match the south aisle. The church was extended by twenty-three feet - two bays – westwards, and a window and doorway were introduced into the new west wall. The old vestry was removed from the south-east side and a new one was erected with an organ chamber opening directly into the south aisle. The former gallery was not replaced and the nave roof was raised considerably. All the monuments were removed and stored before work began and these were later repositioned on the new plaster-free walls. The old pews, complete with doors were removed and replaced with those in use at present and a warm air heating system was installed "to the satisfaction of Mr Middleton, architect." Further additions and alterations were made under Middleton's supervision in the following years again as funds became available. The position of the new organ chamber proved to be unsatisfactory and the organ was removed to the north aisle in 1871 which enabled the vestry in the south aisle to be enlarged. New chancel furnishings were provided at about the same time.

While the work was progressing at Leckhampton, *The Cheltenham Examiner* and *The Builder* reported that an extensive addition was being made to the chancel of St Luke's Church under the supervision of the architect, Mr John Middleton. *The Cheltenham Examiner* called the work 'unusual' in that it was the only known example in the town of the enlargement of an existing church, which required formal consecration. This is explained by the fact that the extension would include that part of the church where the Holy Communion would be celebrated. The church had been designed by the London architect Frederick Ordish and was consecrated in 1854. The work which Middleton was called upon to carry out just twelve years later was the lengthening of the chancel and chancel aisles to provide a further one

Fig. 28 Cheltenham, St Luke

hundred seats. The contract also included the repositioning of the pulpit and the removal of the organ from its position in the west gallery to a new position in the north chancel aisle, beyond which a new vestry was to be constructed.

The east end of the church was demolished and the building was extended about twenty feet towards the present College Road. Additional windows were inserted in the lengthened chancel aisles and in the chancel itself, the latter having marble columns and moulding with hollow moulded hoodmoulds with headstops. The new east window was of an elaborate design and the arch was enriched in typical Middleton fashion with carved Forest stone. On the north and south walls of the chancel were some delicate and attractive floral carvings depicting lilies, primroses and lilies of the valley. Above these ran a frieze of decorated inlaid coloured stone. Within the sanctuary, the east and side walls were ornately decorated with arcades and pinnacles containing mosaic panels on black marble plinths. These panels displayed the symbols of the evangelists. The actual reredos designed by Middleton, was formed of a gabled arcade on a coloured marble plinth and a banner was displayed carved with "Do This in Remembrance of Me." The panels within the arcading had the faces of the four evangelists with that of Christ in the centre. Unfortunately much of the stone that we see today has been painted at some later date. The carving was done by John Roddis of Birmingham and bears a striking resemblance to his work for Middleton at Holy Apostles. The sanctuary also contained an ornate sedilia to the south and a piscina in the north wall. The host of angels which adorned the sanctuary, would have immediately attracted one's attention. Each angel holds a different but easily recognisable musical instrument. This must surely count as one of Middleton's most visually satisfying smaller alterations and deserves wider recognition.

The year 1866 also saw the need for major restoration work at the medieval church dedicated to St Giles at Coberley just a few miles east of Cheltenham. An assessment by the newly appointed incumbent the Reverend Charles Henry Wilson, revealed the need as he saw it, for a complete rebuilding of the chancel and nave and a restoration of the tower and also the fourteenth century chantry chapel. Clearly the church had been neglected for many years and was in a serious state of disrepair. A faculty was granted for the proposed work and between the year 1868 and the completion of the work in 1871, Middleton made approximately twenty site visits to Coberley. The chancel was demolished and rebuilt, "all stone used was rose in the neighbourhood." The roof was renewed and the many carved angels in the sanctuary and chancel carried the emblems of the Passion of Christ. These were the work of R. L. Boulton. On the south chancel wall, Middleton placed the small monument to Giles of Berkeley who had died in 1294 and whose heart was said to be buried in the chancel. This monument had previously been on the north wall. At the same time, he removed an impressive monument with recumbent effigies from the chancel to a new position in the chantry chapel where it can still be admired today. The nave roof was restored, the windows repaired and made uniform, "all according to the old order of architecture" and the best Newcastle glass was used. The arcading separating the nave from the chantry chapel was decorated with richly carved capitals of realistic ferns, acorns and much fine figure carving, which according to David Verey, "reveal Middleton's best Early English design." He also restored the chantry chapel itself and provided a new font to replace the Norman one! The church was reopened for worship in August 1871. In view of Middleton's regular supervision of the work and his apparent commitment to restoration rather than renovation, it is surprising that so little of the Norman church remains today. The Norman font and ancient woodwork have all gone with no record existing of their whereabouts. However having made that observation, it must be admitted that without doubt, his work at St Giles must rank highly among his smaller church successes.

Not all of Middleton's restoration work involved demolition on the scale so far witnessed at Leckhampton and Coberley. Although Coberley is his only known Cotswold commission most of his work in other parts of the county was completed on what one might call clusters, either churches or houses in a particular part of the county, centred in or near a particular town. However before considering some of these, it might be as well to look at the remaining restorations with which he was involved in the immediate vicinity of Cheltenham. Some are more extensively documented than others and a casual visit by Middleton or Goodman recorded in the firm's books, or correspondence, or even drawings and plans, does not always indicate that work was actually carried out. In many cases confirmation has been discovered in parish archives, published parish histories or press reports. This was very much so with the work done at Coberley and was again the case with the work which he carried out on the church at Badgeworth, some four miles south of Cheltenham.

The Church of the Holy Trinity, Badgeworth, is a building of stone in the Decorated style with an embattled tower at the west end. It has a north aisle chapel with a mass of ball and flower decoration around the windows and door. The incumbent, the Reverend A. W. Ellis, who served the parish from 1849-1902, consulted Middleton in 1867-1868 about repairs to the chancel and parts of the nave. Middleton undertook a thorough survey and concluded that compete rebuilding of the chancel was necessary. Work began in 1868 and the new chancel was made much wider than the original and was separated from the nave by a low wall. The floor level was raised both in the chancel and in the sanctuary and a new vestry was provided with an entry through the south wall. The chancel ceiling was panelled and the beams on either side were supported by corbels of beautifully carved angels playing musical instruments or holding inscribed medallions. These all bear striking resemblance to those seen in many of Middleton's other churches. Choir and clergy stalls were supplied at the same time and probably also the nave pews. His final contribution to the restoration of Badgeworth was the rebuilding of the south porch.

A much more important project was completed at Charlton Kings Parish Church in the 1870s. St Mary's is a twelfth century church in the centre of the village and the recently appointed incumbent the Reverend Charles Dundas described the church on his arrival, as "very ugly, very uncomfortable and very badly ventilated." At the Easter Vestry meeting in 1876 Mr. Dundas announced that a restoration committee had been appointed and that the professional services of the well-known architect, John Middleton, had been called upon.

Three phases of the work were identified: work on the body of the church, reseating, and work on the chancel and transepts. The Vestry accepted the proposals and also gave their assent to further discussions which would eventually lead to the complete restoration of the church. Middleton expressed his opinion that work ought to start as soon as possible, as the roof needed to be replaced before winter if the church was to continue to be used while work was proceeding. A faculty was immediately applied for, detailing the extent of the work envisaged. This included restoration and enlargement according to the plans and specifications produced to the committee; tablets as may be requisite to be re-sited, corpses re-interred in other parts of the churchyard and a piece of land on the west side of the church, 18 feet by 60 feet to be enclosed and built upon. His detailed specification which accompanied the faculty application is a good example of the attention he paid to good order and to the personal feelings of those who would be affected by the upheaval.

The proposed work did not receive unanimous approval from parishioners, objections centring mainly on the rights of pew holders, the disturbance of family graves and the quality of the materials to be used. In response to these objections, Middleton assured the committee that he personally would act as clerk of works and that, "No monument will be moved unless absolutely necessary and if moved will be re-fixed on completion of the work. Any graves in or near the foundations will be dealt with as in the specification – that is the bodies will be re-interred." The following month, March 1877, the objectors withdrew their objections and notified the bishop of their decision.

The first phase of the work involved the removal of the galleries, the vaults beneath the floor were filled in and a new concrete floor was laid. The corpses that were buried in graves that would be affected by the proposed extension of the west end were exhumed and re-interred at the south west corner of the extended churchyard. Within a year, the first phase of the work had been completed and Bishop Ellicott presided at the opening of the larger and renewed church on St Mark's Day 1878. The parishioners were encouraged by the beauty of the restoration so far. The removal of the galleries, the new open pews, the panelled, arched ceiling, the new pulpit which had been designed by Middleton and the restored font were all singled out for praise. Although the façade of the extended west end received much admiration, "an extension totally in keeping with the antiquity of the building," Middleton had in fact completely destroyed the original twelfth-century doorway, replacing it with the present gothic one. All that he did retain from the former west front were the gargoyles and the rose window of 1824. However the Bishop remarked that it was the most successful restoration he had seen and even regretted that the nave had not been extended a little further.

In reply to the many public compliments he received at the celebration banquet which followed, Middleton said that when he had taken Lord Lyttleton to visit the church prior to the restoration, his Lordship remarked that it was "a very useful church for it contained everything that ought to be avoided!"

By June 1878, the chancel had been demolished and rebuilding had started along the lines of the original foundations. New windows were inserted in the south and north walls as well as a new three-light east window. This allowed more light into the church as the window glass remained uncoloured until the early 1880s. The roof was raised, an oak panelled sedilia was installed and all the monuments were repositioned, mainly in the nave. The opening of the new chancel took place in November 1878.

The Reverend Mr. Dundas left the parish in 1883 but at that time, the third phase of the work had not been completed due to lack of funds. His successor however was able to authorise Middleton to proceed with the tiling of the aisles, the rebuilding and lengthening of the north transept and the restoration of the ceiling in the south transept. Further work in this transept had to be put on hold.

St Mary's was one of Middleton's most challenging restorations and one for which he received most opposition from parishioners. Some of his work still courts controversy even today, particularly the removal of the plaster from the walls, the removal of monuments from their original positions and the seeming lack of respect for the church's antiquity and the craftsmanship of former generations. This blatantly flouted the *Royal Institute of British Architects Restoration Guidelines* to which he had once adhered so meticulously and casts a shadow over what he achieved at Charlton Kings.

At about the time he was working at Charlton Kings, Middleton was approached to undertake a survey of Holy Trinity Church in Cheltenham with a view to internal reordering rather than structural restoration. Holy Trinity Church was built 1820-1823 in the gothick style with provision for burial vaults and a small burial ground around the outside. Consecrated in April 1823, it was a copybook example of the simple preaching-box with little ornamentation, an insignificant sanctuary area and no chancel. The focus of attention was the pulpit and large galleries occupied three walls with seating for three hundred and seventy people. Middleton's inspection drawings showed a large raised pulpit positioned immediately in front of the shallow sanctuary, the altar was placed against the east wall and the altar rail was concave. The aisle pews were in closed blocks facing inwards towards those in the nave and provided further seating for five hundred and twenty-two people.

Middleton's proposals were dramatic to say the least, but were nevertheless accepted with only a few minor changes. A larger and more identifiable sanctuary was provided with a convex rail. A new, less intrusive pulpit was moved nearer to the west aisle and a freestanding reading desk was installed for the priest. New pews were provided and arranged so that they faced the altar, with the exception of two blocks of inward facing pews near the pulpit and reading desk. These gave the semblance of, but did not actually constitute, a chancel. Tenders were invited by Middleton in May 1877 when the estimated cost of the work was put in the region of £1,748. The following year a further sum had to be raised for additional windows. The galleries were not completely rebuilt as he had originally planned but the front panelling was renewed.

Today, the church has been re-ordered beyond recognition and very little of what Middleton accomplished can now be identified. However, what he did not do is to his credit - the memorial tablets are still in-situ on the plastered walls.

Minor works in the immediate vicinity of Cheltenham were carried out at Swindon Village Church in 1868, where an organ chamber was created and the chancel was retiled and refurnished. There is scant documentary evidence of this work in the archives as it was completed before Goodman joined Middleton in partnership as during that time, plans and drawings do not seem to have survived. A similar story applies to Boddington where Middleton probably carried out restoration work in 1876 which included the removal of the plaster from the nave walls and the design of a new pulpit.

Middleton may also have been responsible for the restoration work at Staverton c1871 and Alan Brooks credits him with the restoration and partial rebuilding of Elmstone Hardwicke Church between 1871-1878.

Although not mentioned in the Middleton files at Gloucestershire Archives, there exists in the Cheltenham Parish Church archive a rather amateurish plan for the 'rebuilding of the Parish Church of Cheltenham' which was being considered in 1863. *The Ecclesiologist* expressed its horror at any proposal to enlarge or rebuild the ancient church but enquiries were received from all over the country and included architects whose names are highly respected in the world of church architecture even today. These include Alfred Bucknall, George Gilbert Scott, G. E. Street, F. W. Ordish and Pritchett and Son of Darlington. The latter were Middleton's father-in-law and brother-in-law, his former partner. Middleton too submitted a design for the rebuilding of the church and one can but question his reason for so doing. The actual plan he submitted bears no comparison with the plans submitted by the other interested parties and in size, detail and accuracy Middleton's appears quite amateurish. He proposed demolishing the church, rebuilding it further to the west almost on the site of the Children's Library of today, to provide an apsidal east end, north and south transepts, north porch and northwest tower and spire. No legend is attached to the plan and needless to say his plan was not accepted - nor were any of the others. Surprisingly, Middleton was not involved at all with St Matthew's Church, apart from presenting the font to the church as his personal gift.

Sources consulted:

Brooks, Chris, and Saint, Andrew: *The Victorian Church*, for The Victorian Society.

Miele, Chris: *The Restoration of Victorian Churches*, for The Victorian Society.

Blake, Steven, *Cheltenham Churches and Chapels*. 1979.

GA, P198. **St Peter's Church, Leckhampton**.

Barnard, L. W: *St Peter's Church, Leckhampton*. c1930.

Miller, Eric: *The History of Leckhampton Church*. 1987.

Andrew, Eve & Brewin, Eric: *Leckhampton Through The Ages*. 1984.

GA, D2970 3/1 **St Luke**, Cheltenham.

Listed Building Description. St Luke's Church, Cheltenham. 14/12/83.

GA, P105; D2970 1/37 & 1/224 & 1/225; 2/2 and 3/9. D843 4/1; **Coberley Church**.

Atherton, Eva: *Coberley, A History of the Church and Village.* 1994.

GA, D2970 3/9 **Badgeworth Church**.

Bradley, C; *Badgeworth Church and Its Village.* 1972.Cheltenham Local Studies Library 25G 726.5 R34663.

Charlton Kings Local History Society Journals, especially No 14 **St Mary's Church**, Charlton Kings.

Paget, Mary: *A History of Charlton Kings*, 1989.

GA, Gloucester Diocesan Records F1/1/1877/1 St Mary's Church.

GA, D2970 1/26 St Mary's Church.

GA, P76 St Mary's Church.

GA, P78/4, and D2970 3/1, **Holy Trinity Church**.

GA, GDR F1/1/1877/5 Holy Trinity Church.

Verey, David and Brooks, Alan: *The Buildings of England. Gloucestershire* 2. **Elmstone Hardwicke.**

GA, P53. **Boddington Church**.

GA, P78 St **Mary's Church, Cheltenham**.

Sawyer, John: *Cheltenham Parish Church and Its Architecture*. 1903.

The Ecclesiologist Vol 24 1863 p152.

Norman, George: *The Provincial Grand Lodge of Gloucestershire*. 1911.

CHAPTER IX

The Cheltenham Colleges

It might seem from what has been written so far that most of Middleton's Cheltenham work was limited to ecclesiastical contracts, but this is far from the truth. With the increasing number of comfortably well-off residents in the town during the 1830s-1840s, it soon became obvious that there was a serious need to provide a good but not too exclusive school for their offspring. In response to the efforts of several retired residents, mainly East India Company and military personnel, Cheltenham College was founded in 1840 and within two years was firmly established on its present site in the Bath Road. Its success was widely recognised and in the 1860s it began what Bryan Little called, "a somewhat unaesthetic career of architectural expansion." It was at about this time that Middleton and his wife and son settled in the town, and in 1861, at the age of fourteen, young John Henry entered College as a day boy.

In 1862, the College Principal was keen to provide facilities for a junior department and although he envisaged a new building, the College Council was more cautious and voted in favour of adapting one of the existing buildings. By the end of the

Fig. 29 Cheltenham College Junior School

Fig. 30 Cheltenham College Junior School

year, the local architect W. H. Knight had converted one of the classrooms and provided a separate entrance and playground for the boys. Within a year this provision was found to be totally unsuitable as the classroom was poorly ventilated and far too noisy. To the Principal's delight, in March 1865, John Middleton was asked by the Council to design a new junior building to the south of the main building. This was opened with 112 pupils on roll by the end of the Midsummer vacation in 1866, and Knight's converted classroom was restored to its original use as the drawing room.

Middleton's junior department was constructed in the Perpendicular style and originally consisted of one large room, 115 feet long, under a steep, pitched roof, surmounted by a fleche. Internally the ceiling was ornamented with pierced panels. A further semi octagonal classroom was added on the side towards the Bath Road and there was also another classroom and the Headmaster's room on the ground floor. The entrance consisted of a small square tower with, above the entrance door, a carved stone figure. Stairs inside the entrance led to the library on the first floor. The building certainly made an attractive addition to the original college although the interior has been much altered since it was opened.

As well as designing this addition to the College buildings, Middleton was also the designer of one of the College boarding houses, Cheltondale. This stood at the corner of College Road where the Hospital Pathology Laboratory is sited, today, almost opposite the east end of St Luke's Church. It was a large and functional building, similar in design to a further three designed by W. H. Knight, all consisting of a master's house, common room, hall, senior boys' studies, dormitories and facilities, but each had its own character and appeal. Although Cheltondale was completed in 1869, Middleton was closely involved in later years with alterations, additions and maintenance

Fig. 31 Cheltenham College House, Cheltondale

to what eventually numbered nine such houses. Many members of the College Council during this period were well-known members of Cheltenham society and became, civic or social associates of Middleton.

Another educational institution was established in the town just before Middleton's arrival but its present buildings in the centre of Cheltenham owe much to Mid-

Fig. 32 Cheltenham Ladies College, the original building

dleton's design. Cheltenham Ladies' College began life in 1854 as a proprietary school for children from local middle-class families. It was located in Cambray House, between the Promenade and Bath Road. When a new Principal, the celebrated Miss Dorothea Beale, arrived in 1858 she found only sixty pupils on the register. She introduced provision for boarding pupils and by 1871 the school was too small for the numbers seeking admission. A new site was purchased on the corner of St George's Road and Montpellier Street and to this was eventually added the site of the Old Well Gardens. In time Fauconberg House and its estate on the corner of Bayshill Road was purchased and this became the first College owned boarding house.

Middleton was called upon to draw plans for the new school and his designs, dated 1871, provided for the original College building, which is now entirely swamped within the present campus, together with a residence for the Principal. By the end of October of that year a loan of £3,000 had been secured enabling the work to be started. The first range together with the Principal's house were completed between 1871 and 1874. Some locals thought the Gothic style which he used, "spired, apsed and generally ecclesiastical in its mien," absurdly grandiose. The school block was faced with Cotswold stone and internally the walls were lined with buff or red bricks with lines of black or blue or very occasionally green, bricks. *The Cheltenham Examiner* urged the College Council to make something memorable of the official opening, by inviting a member of the Royal Family to perform the ceremony, but this did not materialise. However, at the first morning Assembly in the new buildings on 17th March 1873, Miss Beale addressed a small gathering of friends, staff and pupils as follows:

"Some say our school is churchlike...As each stone stands here in its appointed place, resting on one stone, supporting others, so are we a little community, a spiritual

Fig. 33 Cheltenham Ladies College, with Miss Beale's House

Fig. 34 Cheltenham Ladies' College

building: each is placed in her own niche, each has her appointed place, appointed by the Spiritual Architect; each is needful for the perfection of His design."

The new buildings were certainly an improvement on the plain rooms of Cambray House, and the staff and pupils must have been delighted with the patterned interior stonework, the flowers in the coloured glass and the size of the rooms. However there were letters of concern from some parents worried about the draughtiness of the place. The Principal's house was completed in 1874 and by the end of that year it would seem that pupil numbers had reached somewhere in the region of three hundred. Middleton was soon called upon to design the first extension to his original college and Miss Beale was heavily involved in discussing her vision for it with him. Nevertheless, what she wanted and what the College Council thought desirable were not one and the same thing and she had to fight hard and long to achieve her aims.

Fig. 35 Cheltenham Ladies' College

The extension, situated between the south of the original building and Miss Beale's house was completed by 1876 and comprised what is now the Tower entrance, a calisthenics room - for gymnastics - and beyond that a large room with a rose window and a pierced and decorated wooden arch-braced ceiling. At some distance from the main building Middleton designed a Sanatorium which was completed in 1878/9. This was situated just below the junction of the Old Bath Road and Leckhampton Road, at the foot of Leckhampton Hill, and today occupied by Liddington Close. It served as a Sanatorium until 1895. Later sale particulars for this property indicate a substantial premises, rather gloomy in appearance, the Tudor style chimneys being the only attractive feature.

Within two years, further additions were made to the main College buildings. An Art and Music block was commissioned as an extension to the Tower building of 1876 and stretched at right angles to the original building in the direction of Bayshill Road. This wing was to become the main block of the College and was enhanced by additional ornamentation in the early French style. The most striking feature was the entrance hall and Great Staircase – truly in keeping with the importance of the institution. The official opening took place at the beginning of July 1883 when in the evening, Miss Beale gave a reception for a thousand guests, who "added life and beauty to the scene as they toured the buildings and were unstinting in their admiration of the interior." Among the guests mentioned by name were Mr. Middleton the architect and his wife, Mrs Middleton.

Middleton's final contributions to the main Ladies College campus were the Lodge in St George's Road, together with alterations to the Principal's House and some science laboratories which were built facing Montpellier Street, all completed by 1883. However the Middleton practice continued to serve as architects to the Cheltenham Ladies' College until at least 1894.

Fig. 36 Cheltenham Ladies College-showing post-Middleton addition

Fig. 37 Cheltenham Ladies College, St Hilda's

At the time of completion of the new Art and Music wing, Middleton was approached by the College Council to design St Hilda's College in Western Road. Miss Beale wished to provide formal training for Secondary School teachers, which at the time was not available and in response to this initiative, Middleton designed a Students' Home for girls who intended to teach. The foundation stone was laid on 10th August 1884 in the presence of a small number of members of the College Council, some of the College staff together with some of those students who intended to become teachers. The ceremony was followed by a garden party in the grounds of Middleton's home, Westholme, which was situated only a short distance away. Sadly the architect did not live to see the completion of St Hilda's. The official opening took place on 27th November 1885, just nine months after his death and completion of the contract was supervised by his son and partners. The building is in the Elizabethan style, constructed of red brick with Bath stone dressings and mullioned windows. The extensive frontage on to Western Road was considerably and sympathetically extended at the turn of the century and the interior was the subject of major 'refurbishment and upgrading in 2002.

John Middleton was an elected member of the College Council and a shareholder. As the architect of the College from its arrival in Bayshill, it is rather surprising that the Ladies' College Magazine of the period made only brief mention of his death. The autumn edition of 1885 reported, "With unfeigned regret we record the death of Mr John Middleton, ... and continued by providing readers with the exact text of *The Cheltenham Examiner's* obituary, making no specific mention at all of his vast contribution to the design and execution of what is the permanent home of Cheltenham Ladies'

College. Miss Beale did however pay tribute to him in her published *History of the Cheltenham Ladies College 1853-1904*, when she wrote of the death of Middleton, "the Architect to whose taste and genius we owe a large portion of the College, and Cheltenham, its most beautiful churches. Mr Middleton died after a few days' illness, to the great sorrow of a large circle of friends."

Sources consulted:

Little, Bryan: *Cheltenham.* 1951.

Minutes of The Board of Directors/College Council, by permission of the Headmaster and Council of **Cheltenham College**.

GA, D2970 1/29 & 1/30; D/2790 3/1 & 3/9.Cheltenham College.

Hunter, A. A, (ed) : *Cheltenham College Register* 1841 to 1889.

Lowton, Nicholas: *Cheltenham College Chapel*, for The Cheltonian Society 1996.

Steadman, F. C: *In The Days of Miss Beale..* 1931. **Cheltenham Ladies' College**.

Clarke, A. K: *The History of Cheltenham Ladies' College.* 1953.

GA, D2970 1/84, 3/1, 3/7 & 3/9. D843 4/1.

Raikes, Elizabeth: *Dorothea Beale.* 1908.

GA, D4858 2/4/3. **Ladies College Sanatorium**.

GA, CBR C5/6/1/1 **St Hilda's College** and **Cheltondale**.

CHAPTER X

Delancey Fever Hospital

Middleton's work in Cheltenham was not confined to ecclesiastical and educational commissions. To the south of Cheltenham, in Leckhampton parish, stands a fine example of a Victorian Fever Hospital. Such hospitals were built to halt the spread of diseases such as smallpox, diphtheria, cholera, typhoid and scarlet fever. The country-wide cholera epidemic of 1866 may have prompted the building of Cheltenham's Fever Hospital. It was built to the same design as similar hospitals elsewhere, where small buildings were constructed to which larger ward blocks were added later as need arose.

The need for such a hospital in Cheltenham had been identified as early as 1849 when proposals had been made to build one in the grounds of the newly opened General Hospital. Nothing materialised until 1866 when an eccentric local resident, Miss Delancey, made clear to her doctor that when she died, £5000 of her estate was to be used to provide a fever hospital for the town. Nothing was actually put into writing and after her death one of her heirs contested this oral bequest. In 1870 an appeal was heard in the Court of Chancery which resulted in favour of the legatee, but within a month, he had a change of mind and agreed to comply with the deceased's wishes,

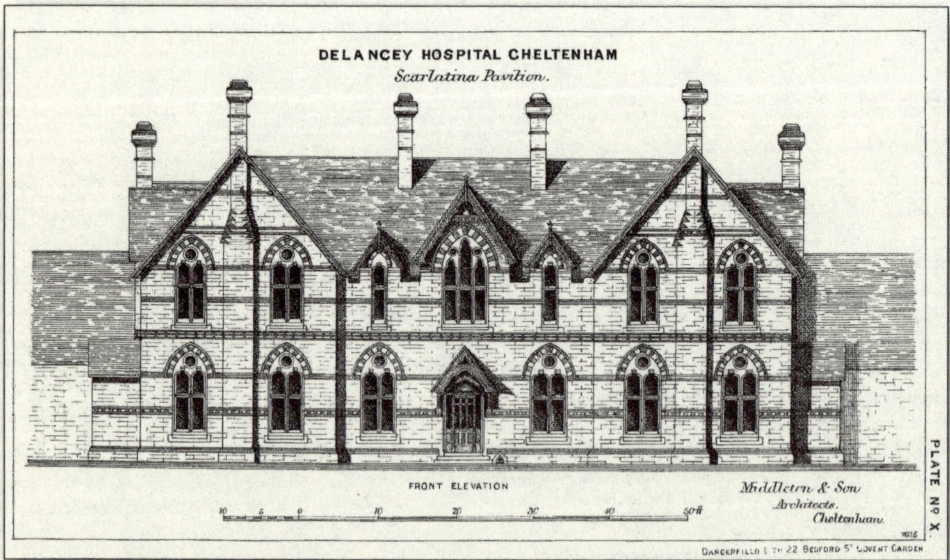

Fig. 38 Cheltenham Delancey Hospital

provided that the hospital bore her name. A local benefactor, the Reverend J. H. Gabell put down £1000 for the purchase of a site at Pilley in Leckhampton and six acres were bought for £1,200. *The Cheltenham Examiner* described the site as a very healthy one, "while it is sufficiently retired to prevent the unnecessary intrusion of the building upon the sight of those who are unwise enough to see in such an institution an object of dread, rather than, as it is, an additional security against the outbreak of an epidemic." The Delancey bequest amounted in effect, to £4,135 but charitable donations began to pour in. A Board of Trustees was appointed and they held their first meeting on 19th May 1871. A sub-committee comprising three doctors and the Reverend Mr. Gabell was elected to deal with the actual building side of the project.

The Trustees agreed to employ the services of an architectural firm which had experience in designing such an institution and by June 1871, outline plans and estimates had been received from the firm of Andrews and Pepper of Bradford. A ceiling of £5,000 had been placed on the project by the Trustees and Dr. E. T. Wilson, secretary to the Trustees went to Bradford to discuss the plans on behalf of the committee. On his return the Trustees raised fifteen points on which they wanted clarification, the most important one being that the proposed cost would be far above the imposed ceiling of £5,000. Mr Pepper was invited to Cheltenham to discuss the Trustees' concerns and he was challenged to find a contractor who would keep within this budget. By March 1872, the lowest tender received was for just over £8,600 and the highest was for nearly £11,000. Again the Trustees emphasised that £5,000 was the limit at which point the architects offered to produce modified plans. The Trustees were not happy and in April of that year, they passed the following resolution:

> "It is resolved that the Trustees having ceased to have any confidence in the Architects therefore cannot countenance to employ them as Architects but will keep their plans and pay a fair remuneration."

Some unpleasant correspondence naturally changed hands but eventually the plans were purchased for £461.4.0 although the copyright remained with Andrews and Pepper of Bradford. A search for a local architect ensued and in May 1872 it was resolved at a meeting of the Trustees that "J. H. Middleton be appointed architect of the proposed hospital." A week later Mr Middleton accepted the appointment and agreed to redraw the plans and work on a 5% commission. This presents us with a very puzzling situation. Which Middleton was the architect - father or son? The archive at Gloucestershire Archives contains several plans for the hospital signed Middleton and Goodman 1872. One undated pen and ink drawing is signed Middleton and Son. The Local Government Board submission to Parliament in 1882 also contains copies of twelve drawings of the hospital plans inscribed Middleton and Son, Architects. It was not until 1876 that Goodman left the partnership and the practice became Middleton and Son and it is more than likely that Middleton senior delegated to his son, John Henry, responsibility for attending some of the meetings and negotiating on behalf of the practice. In not one of the press accounts or minute books before the late 1880s is John

Henry mentioned, all references made being to Mr Middleton or Mr John Middleton. Letters about the work were all written from John Middleton's home, Westholme and are signed 'J Middleton' in his familiar handwriting, whereas John Henry signed his letters J Henry, or John H Middleton or even Henry Middleton.

Things did not proceed as speedily as the Trustees had hoped for and when Middleton laid the received tenders before the Trustees, they were considered too costly and suggested that the whole project be postponed. However the Town's Commissioners intervened and after conferring with the contractors, it was agreed that a cottage style hospital would be the best solution and could still be consistent with the sanitary and heating standards required. Estimates received from Mr Channon were accepted but again a ceiling of £3,500 was placed on the first phase of the project. The deadline set for the opening of what was to be the block for small pox and disinfection, was June 1874 and this was achieved. *The Cheltenham Examiner* clarified the connection between the plans provided by Andrews and Pepper of Bradford and Middleton's final plans. "While preserving the specialities of the plans entrusted to him, Mr Middleton has entirely remodelled their architectural proportions and has prepared a design which, while far more sightly and far less ponderous than the original, will be produced at much less cost." The smallpox block comprised a long building of one storey constructed in locally made brick. All materials used were those least likely to harbour germs. It contained eight beds for general patients in two wards, two private rooms and accommodation for four convalescents, plus a nurses' room and a small surgery. There were additionally all the clerical and domestic offices needed in such an institution. Rooms were airy and spacious, well lighted by gas and well ventilated. A laundry with disinfecting rooms in the basement, stood not far from this block, and at some distance beyond this was a small mortuary.

The cost was in the region of the £3,500 ceiling, and local contractors employed included Debenham and Freebody for the furnishings, Marshall for the window frames, Mallory and Green the hot water system and Letheren the grates for the ward fireplaces.

The opening ceremony was performed by the Rector of Cheltenham and included amongst the invited guests was of course, "Mr John Middleton, the architect." However up to this point, the Delancey legacy had not been touched, the costs having been met by charitable donations. The remaining blocks which had not yet been started would absorb all of the legacy and phase two, the scarlatina block was completed by 1877. It was named after the Reverend Gabell, whose donation of £1,000 had enabled the site to be purchased and who had made further large donations as the work progressed. The boundary walls and gates and the porter's lodge were completed by September 1885, just after Middleton's death; the final stage was completed according to the original Middleton plans, under the supervision of his son, John Henry after 1892. This comprised a new wing for scarlet fever cases, and isolation wards for diphtheria patients. These were named the Wilson and College blocks. At this time the main entrance to the hospital which had been in Pilley Lane was transferred to the present Charlton Lane.

This was by far the largest of Middleton's contracts for public buildings and although it has been enlarged in the twentieth century by Middleton's successors in the practice, most of what he designed is easily recognisable today. However, the first building, the smallpox block has been demolished.

Sources consulted:

Royal Commission on Historic Monuments: English Hospitals, 1660-1948. Pub 1998.

GA, CBR D3/1/1.

GA, D2970 2/2; 3/1; 3/9 No 12.

GA, D2970 11/26; 1/31; 1/53.

The Cheltenham Looker On 26th April 1873; 6th June 1874; 2nd October 1875; 23rd October 1880.

The Cheltenham Chronicle 16th June 1874.

Architects and Survey Plans from the *10th Parliamentary Report of the Local Government Board 1880-1881* on the Infectious Diseases Hospitals in Cheltenham Urban Sanitary District 1881. (Author's collection.)

CHAPTER XI

Private Residences

Tradition has identified several houses in Cheltenham with being to the design of John Middleton. Two of these, Hillfield and The Granleys in St Mark's parish, have been referred to in Chapter V and there is the possibility that a recently demolished property in the same area, Oldfield Crescent, may also have been to his design. Sadly, no plans have so far come to light. However we are more fortunate when it comes to Westholme, Middleton's own personally designed house. It will be remembered that when the family first settled in Cheltenham, they lived at 13, York Terrace in today's St George's Road. Within a matter of six or seven years John Middleton had combined all his artistic and professional skills and designed a home for himself and his family, "the like of which was a complete innovation in Cheltenham's domestic architecture." A one acre site was acquired on the Bayshill Estate and he began the design for his dream

Fig. 39 Cheltenham, Westholme

Fig. 40 Cheltenham, Westholme, the stairway ceiling

house, a French-Gothic pre-Raphaelite Villa, which was to become one of the most elaborate residences in the town. Externally it was not strikingly attractive, being of rock-faced, rusticated stone with freestone dressings. Most of the windows were of two or three lights with Gothic tracery. There was a small pointed oriel on the first floor at the back of the house overlooking Christ Church Road but the main one was on the first floor of the tower above the main entrance, facing north east. The external appearance of the house created an impression of spaciousness which in fact did not really exist. The steep pitched roof and the pointed tower at the front of the house added to its austere and sombre appearance. The frontage to Overton Road was railed and the approach drive was entered between stone pillars.

Internally the house resembled something from an Arthurian legend with beautifully carved stone and plasterwork; Gothic ornamentation; carvings in stone of angels just above eye level; Morris and Burne-Jones tiles around the fireplaces; ceiling panels in Oregon pine, rich and brown-red, with paper transfer work in green, cream and gold. The walls of the rooms were papered and stencilled, possibly to designs by Morris, but they also displayed the skills of the best of Cotswold artists as well as continental, reputedly Italian, craftsmen, such as he employed in the church at Oxenhall, near Newent. The whole effect was Medieval, romantic and sumptuous with some intriguing innovations designed by Middleton himself.

John Middleton with his wife Maria and their son, John Henry, lived here in the house they named Westholme for sixteen years, from 1868. The Census for 1871 indicates that they employed a resident cook, lady's maid and a housemaid although there were probably other non-resident staff also. Caroline, Dowager Countess Dunraven had lunch at Westholme late in 1868 and she later wrote that the architecture of the house was beautiful and "the fittings-up are perfect."

This was not to be Middleton's final Cheltenham address however. In 1884 he sold the property to a client, Mr. A. C. Bruce Pryce, of Duffryn St Nicholas, near Cardiff and just after Christmas 1884 a large advertisement appeared in *The Cheltenham Examiner*:

> "Westholme, Overton Road, Cheltenham. Attractive sale of high class FURNITURE of chaste and elegant design, carpets, choice ornamental items etc. Engal Sanders and Co having received instructions from John Middleton Esq. (who has disposed of the property) to

sell by auction upon the premises as above on Tuesday January 27th 1885 commencing at 11 0'clock precisely....".

There followed an extensive list of "unique items all superior, elegant, handsome, luxurious, elaborate, finely worked." One item typifying the quality of what was for sale was "a noble pitch pine wardrobe of medieval character and superior workmanship." The reader might be tempted to ask what were the circumstances surrounding this important furniture sale. In today's terms, the answer would be 'downsizing'. Middleton was now 65 years of age and the property was obviously too large for just him and his wife Maria as their son, John Henry was now almost permanently resident in London. Therefore in December 1884 Middleton and his wife Maria, purchased Gresham House in St George's Road, which had been first advertised for sale in June of that year.

The actual move to Gresham House took place between the end of 1884 and the beginning of 1885. This property was much smaller than Westholme had been. Although they may have had to sell most of the contents of their larger home, they did take with them its name–Westholme–and this can still be seen in 2006 painted on the west corner of the house in St George's Road. From April 1885, Mr Alan Cameron Bruce Pryce became the owner of the former Westholme and renamed it Abbeyholme.

Fig. 41 Cheltenham Abbeyholme (Westholme) c1900

Fig. 42 Cheltenham Abbeyholme (Westholme) c1900

Alan Cameron Bruce graduated from Exeter College, Oxford, in 1859 and became a Barrister at Law of Lincoln's Inn in 1862. He practised at the Chancery Bar before succeeding to his grandfather's Glamorganshire estate in 1872, a condition of which being that he assumed the additional name of Pryce. For a time he had also been Law reporter for the Times newspaper. Still under fifty years of age when he moved to Cheltenham in 1884, he later became a member of Cheltenham College Council through which he came to know of Middleton, but he never involved himself in local affairs. His descendants have been most helpful in providing descriptions and photographs of the house after Bruce Pryce took it over. It remained in the family's hands until 1945/6 by which time it was too costly to maintain.

One of Bruce Pryce's granddaughters described the house as she remembered it and the following details are a combination of her memories and photographic evidence which her son supplied. Although some minor internal alterations had been undertaken by Bruce Pryce, this description certainly gives the feel of the house during Middleton's occupancy.

"The hall was entered under a Gothic arch, much resembling chancel arches in many of Middleton's churches. This was designed with blocks of alternating blue Forest stone and white Bath stone. On either side of the left hand supporting column were doors leading into the drawing room. The drawing room ran north-east/south-west and leading from it through an arch was the back drawing room and beyond this was

Fig. 43 Cheltenham Abbeyholme (Westholme) c1900

the library although this had been added between 1895 and 1909, some years after Middleton's death. On the opposite side of the hall to the right of the main door was the dining room with an ornate panelled ceiling and a carved stone Gothic fireplace with tiles around the grate. The mantle shelf was castellated and decorated with carved flower heads. On either side of the fireplace was a Gothic arched recess resembling in style an ecclesiastical sedilia. The serving dresser fitted into a square recess on the wall opposite the windows and the top of the recess was supported on two tapered stone bases from each of which rose a short marble column with carved capitals. Nearly all of the woodwork in the house was carved, stencilled or painted. A large, possibly brass, lantern hung from the centre of the ceiling and by the 1930s this had been converted to electricity. Behind the dining room was the pantry and kitchen which one approached by descending a small flight of steps and then almost immediately ascending a similar flight opposite.

Facing one as one entered the hall was a wood staircase at the foot of which slender stone columns with heavily carved foliated capitals supported the first floor landing above. On the first floor landing was a doorway leading into a W.C. and a passage which wandered on and on, turning back or going down steps at most unlikely moments, to a sort of spare room in which was a mahogany panelled bath raised on a small dais and approached by a few steps. The W.C. also set on a small dais, was set in mahogany with a coloured pan. From the landing a further door on the left opened into the oriel room above the dining room, so named because of its big oriel window. Next to this room and facing the top of the stairs was a dressing room for the bedroom next door which was directly above the drawing room. Another door led to a back stairway and eventually up to the domestic sleeping quarters. Bruce Pryce added a wing to the back and side of the house which contained further bedrooms and a W.C. with a bathroom, but compared to the main house this extension was unremarkable."

Fig. 44 Cheltenham Abbeyholme (Westholme) c1970

Photographs of the interior of Westholme taken in Bruce Pryce's occupancy show that the drawing room and the back drawing room were separated by an elegantly carved and stencilled wooden archway. There was a fireplace in each room and a photograph of one in the larger room shows colourful tiles, one of which depicted a dog which reputedly belonged to Middleton himself. In order to encourage the fires to light, there were some black metal hinged flaps which were let down to encourage draughts, very ingenious, and they worked perfectly. Across the front of the fireplace was a screen of steel chains which prevented sparks flying into the room on windy nights. The smaller drawing room had a deep marble mantelpiece backed and surmounted by a huge mirror. The chimney flue was curved instead of vertical and it was always thought odd to have a mirror on a wall so near such a chimney breast. The late Nigel Temple informed me that this mirror in fact hid an exterior window and when a clever device at the side of the fireplace was activated, the mirror ascended to the floor above where it covered the upper chimney breast.

The bathrooms had painted ceilings as did the upstairs oriel room. The ceiling panels in the dining room were also highly decorated. The drawing room wall paper was a light shade of turquoise and had been replaced by Bruce Pryce, but it was an exact copy of the William Morris original.

Miss Audrey Schuster, another granddaughter of Bruce Pryce, recalled living in the house during the 1940s and vividly remembers the glass panels on either side of the inner hall door. One panel bore the legend 'Welcome the coming guest' and the other 'Speed the parting guest.'

Abbeyholme, as Bruce Pryce renamed the house, became a rest home after the Second World War and continued as such until the 1970s. It was not a listed building and in 1973 it was demolished and replaced with flats. Fortunately some of the panelling, interior fittings and stone carvings were rescued by the Bowes Museum and now form part of the furnishings of one of the museum's High Victorian interiors. The

Fig. 45 Abbeyholme (Westholme) the final hour

original front door was salvaged by a local antique dealer and is now an internal door in a house in Cheltenham.

Another house which can definitely be attributed to Middleton was situated on Leckhampton Hill and was named Bartlow. Major Robert Carey Barnard who commissioned the property, was the same age as Middleton and they had similar interests and served on several committees together. Middleton became very friendly with Barnard and was godfather to one of his sons. The house plans are dated 1868 and construction was completed by 1871 although there were later additions. The house was built in a very elevated and commanding position overlooking Leckhampton village for which the Major had a special affection. The external appearance of the house bore a striking resemblance to other houses presumed to have been designed by Middleton. When it was first sold in 1916 the sale particulars emphasise that it was structurally unaltered since it had been first built.

Externally the house was constructed of red brick with decorative bands of dark grey. The roof was steeply pitched with one large projecting gable and two smaller dormer gables. Above the porch was a later stone balcony, the balustrade of which was pierced with trefoil openings which reflected the tracery of the upper floor windows. The property was approached by a steep carriage drive and the entrance to the house was through a massive heavy door leading into a tiled porch. The rooms were large, the downstairs ones having panelled ceilings echoing the ones at Westholme. The two drawing rooms were also similarly arranged to the two at Westholme. The spacious first floor landing had doors leading to six or seven bedrooms of quite sizeable proportions each with its own stone fireplace.

Unfortunately as the result of severe subsidence the house had to be demolished during the 1960s.

Of the other houses reputed to be designed by Middleton, Dewerstone on the corner of College Lawn and Thirlestaine Road in Cheltenham, is one that bears a most remarkable similarity to Middleton's own home, Westholme. The house is an impressive structure of the Gothic revival style and is constructed of stone with ashlar dressings. It has a banded tile and fishscale decorated roof, tall ornamental ridge stacks in twos and threes with cornices and ornamental ridge tiles and end stack. Externally the house comprises two storeys and a basement with attics in the gables. It has three bays with the entrance door set within a projecting gable porch. Above the porch is a triangular oriel window with face decorations. The decorative bargeboards are an unmistakable feature of the house and are something of a hallmark of Middleton's villas. The later extension at the rear of the house bears a date shield for 1871 Above two windows on the west face of the house are carved heads of a lady and gentleman, presumably the Reverend and Mrs Southwood for whom the house was built c1862.

Sale particulars for 1901 enthuse over the internal features, including the stained glass window in the entrance hall, the ornate ceiling cornices in some rooms, massive chimney-pieces in the main rooms, and the wide stone staircase. The handrails are of massive design and the half landing is lit by another stained window. Outbuildings included stables, peach house, vinery, and tastefully laid out pleasure lawns.

Since 1901 Dewerstone has undergone many alterations. The author frequently visited the owner during the 1990s and they discussed Middleton's work in the house. When the house was later sold, the sale particulars attributed its design to "the local architect, John Middleton."

In the north east corner of Wellington Square in Cheltenham stands a residence bearing a remarkable resemblance to Bartlow which was described above and also to the Mythe at Tewkesbury. Although again, the plans for this house have not so far come to light, circumstantial evidence and comparison with known Middleton designs support the theory that this property too, was designed by him. The Cheltenham Borough Register of new buildings for 1867 refers to "a villa in Wellington Square, builders N. C. and L. Channon." A land purchase deed, in possession of the owners of the property in 2001, refers to a house or dwelling now erected by Ellen Bennett and Mary Bennett on the south side of this piece of land, "firstly hereby conveyed and called

Fig. 46 Cheltenham Eastholme

Eastholme." The house is of red brick with ashlar dressings decorated with seven rows of blue brick banding one of which forms an intricate pattern. One enters the house through a pointed plank porch door which still carries its original iron furniture. The porch floor is laid with mosaic red and black tiles. The decorative bargeboards and finials to the several gables are original. Gothic glass panelled doors, Gothic ceiling arches, the Gothic timber staircase, Gothic mullioned windows and the panelled ceiling in the dining room on which can still be seen the remnants of stencilled patterns, all suggest Middleton. The dining room also contains a buffet recess under a Gothic arch identical to the one he designed for Westholme. The drawing room opposite also has a Gothic arch leading into the window bay and an attractive panelled ceiling. The feel of the house and the internal carvings and fittings leave one in little doubt that here we have another of Middleton's domestic designs.

One house that still begs further research is Hetton Lawn at Charlton Kings. An article in *Charlton Kings Local History Journal 10/5* suggests that this building was added to the original Bolton House by John Middleton in 1862. The then owner was the Reverend H. G. Liddell whom Lewis Carroll visited when in Cheltenham and whose granddaughter provided the inspiration for Carroll's 'Alice'. Liddell was one of the local subscribers to the appeal for funds to build the new church in Darlington designed by Middleton at the start of his career and they may well have renewed acquaintance when they met up again in Cheltenham. There is strong probability that Middleton was responsible for the conversion although extant Middleton archives for this period are very sparse and contain no reference to Hetton Lawn let alone Bolton House.

Sources consulted:

Verey, David: *The Buildings of England. Gloucestershire: The Vale and the Forest of Dean.* **Westholme.**

Information about **Westholme,** supplied by Mrs Loraine Maclean, granddaughter of Mr Bruce Pryce; Rev Canon Allan Maclean, great grandson of Mr Bruce Pryce, and Miss Audrey Schuster, granddaughter of Mr Bruce Pryce.

GA, D2970 1/20-127 and 3/7.

The Cheltenham Looker On 18th April 1885 and 15th May 1909.

Information supplied by the late Nigel Temple.

Public Record Office of Northern Ireland. The Diary of the Countess Dunraven. (Ref. Chapter XII)

The Gloucestershire Echo May 29th 1973.

Correspondence with Peter Howell of the Victorian Society.

The Cheltenham Looker On 15th October 1862 ;18th December 1869; 29th December 1906. **Bartlow:**

Barnard, L. W: *Ninety Years Past.* 1949.

GA, D2970 2/2; 3/1; 3/7 and 3/9.

GA, D4858 2/3-1.

Sale Particulars in possession of the author 1998. **Dewerstone.**

Conversations with the former owner 1995-1997.

Verey, David & Brooks, Alan: The Buildings of England: *Gloucestershire, The Vale and the Forest of Dean.*

Morgan, M. C: *Cheltenham College: The First Hundred Years.* 1968.

GA, CBR C5/6/1/1/1. **Eastholme.**

Census Return for Cheltenham 1871.

Sale Particulars in possession of the author 2002.

Listed Buildings Description 1/6/1991.

Conversation with the vendors in 2002 and inspection of 1870 land conveyance.

Visit to the house and conversation with the owners 2002: **Hetton Lawn.**

Charlton Kings Local History Bulletin 10/5.

CHAPTER XII

The Forest of Dean - Clearwell, a Middleton village

With one exception, most of John Middleton's work in Gloucestershire beyond Cheltenham is concentrated on two centres - Tewkesbury and Newent. The exception is the village of Clearwell in the Forest of Dean where our architect was responsible for several buildings shortly after completing St Mark's Church in Cheltenham.

Clearwell was a village and tithing of Newland formed in 1856 into a separate ecclesiastical parish. The story of Middleton's work at Clearwell is interesting in that he was responsible for the construction of two churches in the village, a cottage hospital, a village well-house, the restoration of the village Cross and additions to the village school. He also made modest external alterations to Clearwell Court, now Clearwell Castle, together with more ambitious additions and alterations to the internal fixtures and fittings. All of this work was done at the invitation of the owner of the Court,

Fig. 47 Clearwell, St Peter's Church

Caroline, Dowager Countess of Dunraven and Mount Earl, whose diaries suggest that she was a personal friend of John Middleton as well as a professional client.

Fig. 48 Caroline, Dowager Countess Dunraven

Clearwell Court dates from c1730 and was inherited by Thomas Wyndham of Dunraven Castle, Glamorgan. On his death it passed to his son and then to his granddaughter, Caroline. She married the Honourable Windham Henry Quin in 1810 and in 1815 they assumed the surname Wyndham in addition to and before that of Quin. Windham Henry Wyndham-Quin's father was given an Earldom in 1822 and he took the title Dunraven from his daughter-in-law's family seat in Glamorgan. In 1824, on the death of his father, Windham Henry became Wyndham-Quin, the second Earl of Dunraven. He and his wife Caroline spent most of their married life happily restoring the family home, Adare Manor in County Limerick. On his death in 1850, Caroline became Dowager Countess of Dunraven and Mount Earl. After the death of their daughter Charlotte five years later, Caroline decided to return to the place of her birth, Clearwell Court in the Forest of Dean where she lived from 1857 until her death in 1870.

During the time the Countess lived in Ireland prior to the death of her husband, the Court suffered from serious neglect. On her return to Clearwell, she set to work immediately to make the family seat habitable, using local labour and resources. She then engaged Middleton to undertake extensive works of restoration, additions, decoration and furnishings. His ledgers give some idea of the range of work for which he was engaged: erection of additional rooms, design of a conservatory, repairing floor beams throughout the Court, decoration of the dining room, entrance hall and staircase, decoration of dressing rooms and bedrooms, general structural repairs, and designs for furniture for the dining room, entrance hall, bedrooms etc. In some of this work he employed the services of his son, John Henry especially in the design of the furniture

Fig. 49 The Monogram of the Countess Dunraven

Fig. 50 Clearwell, St Peter, the pulpit

and fittings such as classical chimney-pieces and compartmented ceilings and cornices.

Until 1866 the old church at Clearwell which was surrounded by a graveyard, stood at the Coleford end of the village and served as a chapel-of-ease to Newland. The Countess's made many references in her diaries for 1863 to evenings spent with Middleton discussing amongst other things, her ideas for a new church at Clearwell. These references continued into the following years and frequently Middleton stayed overnight so that an early start could be made the following day to visit proposed sites for a new church, hospital, castle lodges, well or school. On some days the Countess spent the whole day accompanying him on these visits and she recorded how much it pleased her to see the vast amount of work he had done and how well he had done it. Although the diaries do not give a lot of detail about what was discussed, the Countess's input and interest are quite evident. She had petitioned the Diocese of Gloucester for the demolition of the old chapel-of-ease, for a faculty for a new church on a new site and for the parish to be declared an independent Vicarage. In 1866 she was able to rejoice in having achieved her aims and she was made Patroness of the new Living and the new church of St Peter was consecrated on 5th April 1866.

The site chosen for the new parish church was in the centre of the village, opposite the school and close to the main entrance to the Castle. It was built of red sandstone with white Bath stone dressings and was in the French Gothic style of the 13th century. Like its contemporary in Cheltenham, St Mark's, it was completed with tower and impressive spire which soared one hundred and twenty feet heavenwards. Today one enters the church through a wooden porch with heavy framing and highly decorative barge boards. The four bay arcades on either side of the nave are supported on piers of blue and white stone bands with moulded bases and richly foliated capitals. As in many of Middleton's other churches, Clearwell boasts a goodly company of carved angelic figures in its internal decoration. As one moves up the nave, one is aware of the moulded archway leading into the Chancel above which are two medallions bearing the symbols Alpha and Omega. Between these medallions is a

Fig. 51 Clearwell, St Peter, the Reredos

Fig. 52 Clearwell Church interior

richly carved and foliated cross with passion flower terminations to the four extremities. The chancel itself is richly and colourfully decorated and within the Sanctuary, the reredos, once again, carved by John Roddis of Birmingham, displays red and green marble shafts, enriched arches and gables and inlaid marble crosses. The piscina and sedilia match the decoration of the reredos and there is an abundance of marble from Ireland, Italy and Derbyshire. The reredos was given by the Countess' daughter-in-law in memory of her late husband, the Countess' son, who had died in 1865. The daughter-in-law was related to the Tylers of Mount Gernos in Cardiganshire for whom Middleton completed work between 1869 and 1877 which is described in Chapter XX.

The organ which originally came to Clearwell from the family home in County Adare in 1866, was moved to the church from the Court and the Countess recorded in her diary for the year 1869 how she had attended church and heard the organ played there for the very first time. St Peter's Church is a unique Middleton memorial in that it has remained undisturbed by succeeding generations and is very much as Middleton designed it. The moulded ribs to the ceiling still show their gold and coloured decoration and most of the pews still retain their brass candle-light standards.

Just a few hundred yards from the church stands the fourteenth century Village Cross. It had been much mutilated before the Countess came to Clearwell and she commissioned Middleton to restore it at the same time that he was supervising the building of the church. The restored twenty foot high cross is built of grey Forest stone but the steps and shrine of four niches are the only surviving parts

Fig. 53 Clearwell, the Cross

Fig. 54 Clearwell, Cemetery Chapel

of the original structure. Middleton sympathetically restored the upper section in a style in keeping with its original date. This can be seen in the lengthened shaft and the elegant floriated cross which he designed as the finial. In close proximity to this old Cross flows one of the many springs which have long served the inhabitants of the village but which was then subject to pollution and defilement. The Countess invited Middleton to design a very picturesque shelter over this spring which bears the title, St Anne's Well. This attractive little building was ornamented with a bold Gothic arch and fitted with a substantial basin through which the stream's pure, clear water could flow. The water still flows today, and the shelter, or well house, has undergone considerable restoration during 2005.

With the completion of the new St Peter's Church, the site of the former chapel-of-ease was retained as the village cemetery. The chapel was demolished in 1867 and a mortuary chapel was erected in its place. Middleton designed it in the style of the thirteenth century and it contains a fine rose window over the east door together with a small bellcote. The chapel is in a poor state of repair and there has been talk of demolition. This would be a great loss as it is an integral part of Clearwell, the closest we can come to a 'Middleton Village.'

Fig. 55 Clearwell, the Hospital

The work achieved so far - chapel, new church, the village cross and well-house obviously met with the Countess' approval and in 1868, Middleton was approached to design a hospital for the village. Her diary describes how she went with Middleton and her estate manager to look for a site for the hospital and how they found one that they thought would be perfect. The site was just north of the Castle on the other side of the main road. Middleton spent the following weekend with the Countess at Clearwell drawing up plans and making arrangements for the work. Between October 1868 and December 1869, when the hospital was completed, Midleton made twenty-five visits to Clearwell. William Beach was given the building contract with Letheren and Marshall of Cheltenham supplying the fittings and heating system. The hospital was very similar in design to the one Middleton was responsible for at Tewkesbury. There is some doubt however whether it was ever actually used for the purpose for which it was built. Today the building has been converted into a private dwelling, enlarged, but retaining some of the original internal features.

Middleton was also responsible for extending the village school which stands opposite the church but this was not a significant addition to his work in the village. Sadly the Dowager Countess did not live long enough to fully enjoy the many amenities she had provided in the village she obviously loved so dearly. She died at the Court on 26th May 1870 and her body was later transported to Ireland where after a period of lying in state in Adare Manor she was buried alongside her husband in the Quin family vault in Adare Parish Church.

During the time that he was occupied at Clearwell, Middleton also submitted a design for a new church in the neighbouring town of Coleford. Whether his plans were too ambitious or funds were not available we cannot tell but after 1871 there is no further mention of Coleford in his ledgers. A new church was eventually built there in 1880, but it was to the design of the Gloucester Diocesan Architect, F. S. Waller.

Sources consulted:

Public Record Office of Northern Ireland D/3196/E 2/1-68; D/3196/E/2/67;MIC/646/5. Years 1863 – 1869, Diaries of the **Countess Dunraven**.

The Gloucester Chronicle 4th June 1870 p3.

GA, D2970 2/2; 3/1; 3/9 No 3 and No 7.

GA, P88 CW 3/1; P88 IN/3/6; P88 IN/3/1.

The Builder 7th April 1866.

The Church Builder Vol. 20.

Pooley, Charles, FSA: *Old Crosses of Gloucestershire*. 1868.

GA, D1430b/28 Bruton Knowles archive 1908 – Clearwell Castle.

Kingsley, Nicholas: *The Country Houses of Gloucestershire, Vol. II* pp104-105. 1992.

GA, D2970 1/38.

Country Life article on **Clearwell Castle** Oct/Dec 1995.

Harris's Forest of Dean Almanack 1912.

The Illustrated Times. Feb 16th 1867.

CHAPTER XIII

Work in Newent and the surrounding area

Newent, a small town a few miles west of Gloucester. It has a fine fourteenth century church and a seventeenth century market hall. One of the town's most documented historical families is that by the name of Wintour. They were ardent Royalists during the Civil War and owned lands in the Forest of Dean together with an extensive estate in the town of Newent and a house there, named Stardens. Stardens passed from the Wintours to the Foley family and, by marriage in the nineteenth century, to the Onslow family. At the time of Middleton's involvement with Stardens, it was owned by Richard Foley Onslow, who was deeply conscious of his exalted position in the locality and spent his money freely. His fortune had been made from working the coal and iron deposits which were to be found on the estate.

Richard Foley Onslow decided to make modest Stardens a worthy seat for a Victorian country squire. The old house was neither large nor architecturally remarkable and Onslow consulted Middleton in 1863-1864 about his vision to transform the property into a Gothic style mansion. At the time the house comprised a detached

Fig. 56 Stardens, Newent

three storeys residence of three bays under a steeply pitched roof. Middleton designed the conversion around the original house adding two new large wings in Gothic style, one either side of the house to form an irregular H-plan. Today, the south elevation gives the best view of the original house where all its windows were altered to Gothic and a gabled bay on each side indicates the extent of the addition. The west bay has an impressive triangular oriel window centrally placed under a cusped circular window but the east wing is even more impressive with its single storey square bay with very elaborate tracery and heraldic animals on the upper corners. Internally many of the rooms boasted large stone and marble fireplaces, panelled ceilings, carved stone corbels to support the ceiling timbers and ornate cornices. Richard Foley Onslow almost bankrupted himself in creating this Gothic mansion and his heir, his son Andrew, was forced to sell the house in 1913. It has in recent years served successively as a nightclub, a country club and in the year 2000 it was converted to provide private apartments.

Only a couple of miles away from the centre of Newent, and even closer to Stardens, is the parish of Oxenhall. Richard Foley Onslow of Stardens was responsible for employing the services of John Middleton in a major restoration of this parish church, a seventeenth century rebuild of a fourteenth century original. The whole building was in a dreadful state of repair and urgent repairs to the tower and spire were immediately approved by the Vestry Meeting in 1865 with the agreement that when funds became available, the nave and chancel would be rebuilt. Work began in 1866 and Middleton's designs amounted in effect to a total rebuilding apart from the tower and spire. The rest of the building was demolished and rebuilt, using much local stone quarried from a site to the east of the church where the present car park is now situated. The church stands in a prominent position and has a western buttressed tower, a

Fig. 57 Oxenhall, St Anne's Church

south porch and a north-east vestry. Internally there is much carving to be admired - flowers, fruit, leaves, birds and angels holding musical instruments as at Coberley. The reredos was carved by John Roddis of Birmingham as was the tracery of the east window. Most of the remaining stone carving was completed under the supervision of R. L. Boulton, then of Worcester although there is a local legend that Middleton imported Italian craftsmen for some of the work. Mr Baldwin, churchwarden when the author visited the church in 2000, recalled his grandfather telling him that these foreigners were well known in the neighbourhood and especially in the pubs of Newent, where they filled up with liquid refreshment before starting work in the church. Middleton also replaced all the high backed pews with those currently in use.

The church was consecrated by the Bishop of Gloucester in June 1867 although the porch and the carving in the chancel had not yet been completed. The lychgate is also by Middleton and formed part of the original contract. However as at Charlton Kings, Middleton seems to have been ruthless in his destruction and discarding of ancient craftsmanship and this is difficult to understand. The Norman Tympanum above the main door at Oxenhall disappeared during his restoration and has never been found. The upper part of the spire was removed in 1972 and the remainder was removed in 1985.

Towards the end of his career, Middleton and his son were consulted about proposed restoration work on the church of St Mary the Virgin, in Newent. Although the church retained its fourteenth century tower and nave of 1675, St Mary's had undergone severe and extensive alteration by the time that Middleton inspected it. Sir George Gilbert Scott had submitted proposals for the church's restoration in 1878, but presumably these would have been too expensive, for in 1879, the Diocesan Architect, F.

Fig. 58 Newent, St Mary's Church

S. Waller was asked to submit his plans for alterations and restoration. In 1880 Middleton and his son were invited to survey the church and to draw up plans for the Onslow Window at the east end. The east window had fallen out in 1751 and had not been replaced, the gap being merely bricked in. However completion of this window was just part of the work Middleton was eventually contracted to carry out.

His extensive restoration took only a few months to complete and the reopening of the church for worship was celebrated on Thursday 4th December 1884, just before Middleton's death. His work included removing the plaster from the interior walls which were left rough and "securing a handsome and appropriate appearance" according to a contemporary description. However David Verey challenged this in 1965 when he described the church as being horribly scraped of all its plaster by John Middleton "who had an exaggerated feeling for texture." Middleton also altered the old oak seats to a uniform design and removed the pew doors. The plaster ceiling in the nave was replaced with one of panelled wood and the old south aisle chapel was "thoroughly restored, all three architectural styles being maintained in this work of entire conservation." *Gloucestershire Notes and Queries* in its account of the opening, heaped unashamed praise on Middleton, "who deserves credit for the way in which he has restored the church without destroying its special characteristics," an opinion sharply in contrast to that of David Verey.

Further work in Newent was completed by Middleton on a property named Newent Court or New Court, built c1810. Middleton enlarged the service block and provided an extension to the bow window in the dining room so that it extended vertically the full height of the house, and he added a billiard room. The work was completed by 1884 but the house was demolished in about 1970

In the same part of the county, on the road from Gloucester to Hereford is the ancient parish church of St Mary at Dymock. This church too has undergone many restorations and alterations most notably in the mid to late 1800s. Middleton's contributions were more functional than aesthetic and date from the 1870s. The plans submitted by Middleton recommended re-seating and re-flooring the entire church, recovering and reburying any bodies that might be discovered while the work was in progress, and repositioning with them any grave stones or slabs which might be disturbed. Middleton had written a lengthy survey of the building and had highlighted areas that required immediate and urgent attention – including the unwholesome smell when one entered the building, the walls saturated with moisture, the decaying boarded floors under the pews and the poorly covered vaults under the floors which emitted dangerous gasses.

Additional work which was not originally planned but which Middleton considered necessary as work progressed was the complete taking up and then concreting the chancel floor, the stripping of all the wall plaster apart from that in the chancel and repointing the walls, and removing the unsightly gallery. The work took about twelve months, and "a man in the village (has) offered to take down the gallery for nothing," thus saving Middleton's £10 fee.

Dymock is not one of Middleton's most aesthetically pleasing restorations and some would say that it amounted to sheer vandalism, but it addressed the needs of the congregation at a time when these were often neglected.

Work of a more exciting nature was conducted at an ancient parish church, which was situated at a considerable distance from the actual village of Kempley. The church had a twelfth century doorway and chancel arch. A wealth of medieval wall paintings were obscured with whitewash during the Reformation. A new incumbent of Kempley, the Reverend Arthur Hislop Drummond began his ministry in the parish in 1872 and he immediately consulted the patron of the living, the Earl Beauchamp, about the deplorable state in which he found the church. Mr Drummond was authorised to go ahead with whatever work he considered necessary. John Middleton visited the church and recommended that a faculty be applied for in order for restoration work to be undertaken, but within a day or two scraping of the whitewash seems to have begun and a builder noticed colouring beneath the whitewash. The Reverend Drummond recorded in his diary, that within twenty-four days, "the Twelve Apostles are appearing in the Chancel." John Henry Middleton recorded the events leading up to the discovery of the frescoes and they aroused considerable local interest, including that of Mr. Gambier Parry of Highnam who dated them to 1180. Middleton made several visits specifically to examine the frescoes and John Henry and Mr. Young, the firm's clerk of works, copied them. The Reverend Drummond recorded in his diary that John Middleton senior was the chief restorer assisted by his son, but their work was not as competent as John Henry suggested in his later description of the process. Their method of coating the frescoes for preservation was much criticised in later years and the plasterers whom they employed were neither as skilled nor as conscientious as one would have expected. Middleton did complete further survey work on the church and designed a new altar in 1873 but this was overshadowed by the enthusiasm surrounding the discovery of the ancient wall paintings. This redundant church is now in the loving care of the Churches Conservation Trust.

The Kempley Vicarage was another focus for the newly appointed incumbent's attention and in 1873 the Earl Beauchamp authorised the building of a new Vicarage which was completed the following year. Middleton was appointed architect and his visits to the site and house spanned the period April 1872 to May 1873. It is worth noting that in 1886, the Diocesan In-

Fig. 59 Kempley, St Mary's Church

Fig. 60 Kempley Vicarage

spection of Vicarages reported that whilst Kempley Vicarage had been built only twelve years previously an extensive list of repairs was needed to be carried out! The property is no longer the Vicarage and is named Kempley House.

School design was another area in which Middleton contributed to the architecture of the Newent area and he was commissioned to design a parish school for the village of Bromsberrow. The work took considerable time, owing to lack of immediate funds in spite of a grant from the National Society. However the school and master's house was completed by 1871 at a cost of £571. The plans are signed Middleton and Goodman but JM is credited in the firm's accounts with 9/6 for each journey to the site. He also designed a school at Gorsley which was opened just six months later and is a stone, L-shaped building with a bell cote. For some time, the school was also used as the village church. Other school work was completed in the area in 1871-1872 chiefly at Picklenash School in Newent but none of this was of any real architectural interest.

Sources consulted:

Douglas, J.C: *Historical Notes on Newent with Oxenhall*. Gloucester Local Studies Library R212.43. 1912.
Bick, David: *Old Newent and District*. 1992.
GA,D2970 1/131; 2/2; 3/1,9. D1882 5/1 pt 2. D 2593 2/547. PA 225/2. **Stardens and New Court.**
GA, P241 VE 2/1 and CW 3/3. **Oxenhall.**
Conversation and visit with Mr Baldwin, Churchwarden 2000.
Smith, Brian: *Gloucestershire Historical Studies*. University of Bristol Extra Mural Dept. Vol II. 1968.

GA, D2970 3/1.
Listed Building Description. 3/183. 2.10.54.
GA, P225 CW 3/5 and VE 2/4. **St Mary's Church, Newent**.
Gloucestershire Notes and Queries Vol V p189.
Church Guides. Newent St Mary's 1962, and 2000.
O'Connor, Rev. Canon: *Newent St Mary*, Cheltenham Local Studies Library 199G 726.5. 1929.
GA, P125 CW 3/2; CW 3/14; 4/19; VE/24. **Dymock.**
GA, D2970 3/1; 3/9 No 14.
GA, D843 4/1 pp 215,218,235. D843 1/2.
Kelly's Directory for Gloucestershire 1896.
Gethyn-Jones, Rev. J. E: *Dymock, A History of the Church and Parish*. 1967.
GA, D1381/95. **Kempley** Church and Vicarage.
Gethyn-Jones: Rev E: *Kempley and its Paintings* Vol I 1872-1958. 1961.
Woolhope Naturalists' Field Club Journal 1878 p80.
Transactions of the Bristol and Gloucestershire Archaeological Society Vol 10 p247.
The Gloucester Diocesan Magazine 1911.
GA, D1381/95. The former vicarage is now named **Kempley House**.
Rigby, F.F: *To Our Lady of* ***Bromsberrow***, p46. 1970.
GA, D2970 1/78 and 2/2. Other drawings are in D2186/16 and include a Teacher's House.
GA, D2970 2/2; 3/1.
GA, **Gorsley** D2970 3/1 and 3/7.
GA, Gorsley School P155 SC/1/1.

CHAPTER XIV

Tewkesbury and surrounding villages

It is fascinating to see how much of Middleton's work was clustered in particular areas and how, presumably, personal recommendations secured contracts for further work. This certainly was the case with several of the contracts we will look at in this chapter. We begin with the little church at Walton Cardiff of which no trace remains today.

A church dating from the fourteenth century had been rebuilt c1658 and by 1863, this replacement had become so run down and dilapidated that roof tiles were falling through the rafters and the walls were in danger of collapsing. A thorough survey was carried out by Collins, Cullis and James of Tewkesbury and at a subsequent Parish Meeting, the Vicar of Tewkesbury was authorised to approach Mr John Middleton of Cheltenham with a view to engaging him in the design of a new church using where possible the old materials. The building was to be inexpensive, neat, durable, and free from flooding, in consideration of which it was suggested that the church should be built about six hundred yards from the existing building. The proposed site did not

Fig. 61 Walton Cardiff, St James

belong to the church however and so this possibility was not realised. Middleton therefore prepared plans for a new church on the existing site, and he raised the floor level of the new building to prevent flooding. Only two tenders were submitted and a public appeal was started to enhance the existing building fund. John Middleton, as was his custom, was one of the first to subscribe to the appeal. The appeal literature drew attention to the state of the old church, "defective foundations, four walls falling outwards, the roof falling in" and acknowledged that "continuous repairs would be a useless outlay of money."

Work began in November 1867 and within eighteen months the church was completed in the Franco-Norman style and was dedicated to St James. It was built of brick with stone facings on the outside and rendered inside. The ground plan comprised a nave with a wooden screen providing a vestry area at the south-west corner, and a small apsidal sanctuary at the east end. At the north-west corner provision was made for a bell turret. Seating was provided for seventy-three people. Middleton again used the firm of R. L. Boulton for the carved stonework which included deeply carved capitals to the pillars and angels bearing heraldic shields.

For some time prior to 1963 services had been held only once a month and as a result of continual flooding, relocation of the population and increasing dilapidation and vandalism, the church was demolished in 1970. A letter to *The Evesham Journal* in 1972 described how it had "all gone to rack and ruin. Kids had smashed it up and the doors had been left open for cattle to get in, but only a small part of the roof had gone."

At approximately the same time that Middleton was working at Walton Cardiff, he was also engaged in the restoration of the Church of St Mary Magdalene just two miles north of Tewkesbury at Twyning. The Norman church had been altered, repaired and enlarged through the centuries and as late as 1830, the interior had been extensively renovated and the walls plastered. Nearly fifty years later the church was in an unsightly and sad condition. Middleton was engaged to undertake a major restoration to the chancel, the nave and to some extent the tower. He assured the congregation that if his plans were carried out, the church would be "one of the finest of its size in the County of Gloucester." Work began in 1868 and the main focus was the chancel where today, as a result of Middleton's energetic and daring attack, very little of the original remains. Apart from the north-east window, all the others are to his design. The short wall

Fig. 62 Walton Cardiff, St James

shafts with corbels and capitals are carved with deeply undercut foliage, all by R. L. Boulton. The sixteenth century monument was moved to its present position from its original one against the north wall where the vestry door now is. Another memorial, now in the tower, was also situated in the chancel until it was re-sited by Middleton. Thankfully he reused the two medieval corbel heads which one can now see on the east wall of the chancel. He also replaced some of the nave roof beams, the nave floor was re-laid, nave windows were replaced with typical Victorian Gothic ones and the south wall of the nave was rebuilt. The gallery at the west end was dismantled and not replaced. Middleton also designed new furnishings including the pews which reused some of the early oak panelling. The base of the font is to his design as is the pulpit which replaces the original one. This pulpit is not unlike the one at Boddington, which is reputed to be by Middleton.

Twyning was one of Middleton's classic major restorations and will qualify in many people's minds for the accolade which he predicted in 1867. The disciples of 'anti-scrape' however, would see it as terribly invasive.

Another ancient church, St Mary, at Forthampton, is only three miles west of Tewkesbury and here one can again see examples of Middleton's restoration and reordering. In 1866 Joseph Yorke, M.P. and Lord of the Manor, enlisted the help of William Burges to enhance the sanctuary of St Mary's by providing a sculptured reredos, a triple light east window and a rustic altar rail. Middleton's work followed close on that of Burges and by 1869 he had almost given the church the internal appearance which it has in 2005. His main contribution was to enlarge the vestry at the east end of the north aisle, and to open up the north wall of the chancel into this new vestry which he converted into an organ chamber. The organ could then be reached through a newly created arch supported on corbels of groups of finely carved angels all playing musical instruments. The north aisle entrance to this organ chamber was enhanced by means of an elaborate traceried arch. The space under the west tower was converted into a vestry by the addition of an oak screen across its width. The present stone and alabaster font and the stone pulpit were also designed by Middleton. In 1872 he provided the low oak screen wall to the chancel, the choir stalls and oak ceiling but not the unusual chancel arch. The supporting figures of St Peter and St John the Evangelist are to his personal design. Unfortunately his stencilled decoration of the east wall of the sanctuary is no longer visible.

Sir Stephen Glynne visited Forthampton Church in 1871 and remarked that "the church has undergone such frequent and thorough restoration that little of the stone building is of interest to the antiquarian." We shall hear more of his opinion of Middleton's work when we consider the church at Woolstone, a small village approximately six miles east of Tewkesbury. When Glynne visited this church in 1871, it was in the throes of Middleton's restoration: "The church was undergoing new fittings and renovation and the chancel roof was off."

The ancient church of St Martin at Woolstone had been allowed to fall into a dismal state of disrepair and Middleton was engaged to put matters right. The work was designed and supervised by Middleton and his partner Mr Goodman between 1871 and 1873. Externally the work involved rebuilding the tower which was sinking

Fig. 63 Woolstone, St Martin

to the west and south-west and to which extra foundations had to be added. Internally the walls were stripped of their plaster in typical Middleton fashion, the window in the north wall of the nave was filled in and two new windows inserted, the roofs of the nave and chancel were removed and replaced with new ones of pine, but the old stone tiles were reused. All furnishings were removed from the chancel and new pine pews were placed in the nave together with a new wooden pulpit carved by R. L. Boulton. A tower clock was provided anonymously and was in place for the opening ceremony in March 1873 at which John Middleton was named amongst "the respectable congregation." *The Cheltenham Examiner* praised Mr. Middleton in its report of the opening of the restored church "for preserving every item of the original architecture which in any way tends to accentuate the history of the building." This no doubt referred to the two canopied niches either side of the east window, which had been covered up since the Reformation, and which Middleton had revealed and restored. The south porch was added in 1877. Although alterations have been made since Middleton's day, looking eastwards from the back of the church gives one a very good impression of how Middleton's restoration must have looked at the time of completion.

Still in the Tewkesbury area and on the old road from Tewkesbury to Gloucester is the parish of Leigh. The medieval chapel dedicated to St Katherine had naturally undergone several restorations down the ages, the last one before that undertaken by Middleton, being in 1865. The incumbent, the Reverend Mr Gabell, was well known to Middleton through their joint association with Delancey Hospital and St Mark's Church in Cheltenham. When Middleton was asked to consider restoring St Katherine's, it was acknowledged that the church was "inconvenient for the proper orderly conduct of divine worship, unsightly in construction and quite unsuitable for the present age." A faculty for the proposed work according to Middleton's plans was granted in June 1884 but delay in raising funds meant that work was not completed until nine months after the death of John Middleton. The actual work included laying new floors throughout the church, the box pews were replaced with open pews, the tower was separated from the nave by a screen as at Forthampton, and the north porch was reconstructed on the south side of the nave. The window displaced by the move was repositioned where the north door had been. New seats, a new pulpit and a new reading desk were also provided. Later work, just after this initial contract was completed was carried out to underpin the south wall of the nave and the south wall of the tower, and several tombstones were re-sited. One of the most interesting features of the church is the trussed oak roof, which was revealed when the existing plaster was removed during the restoration, but sadly Middleton did not live to see his plans materialise and the work was completed by his son and his partners Messrs Prothero and Phillott. The reopening took place in October 1885.

Not all of his work in the Tewkesbury area was of an ecclesiastical nature however. Hospital provision in the town had begun in 1864 when two cottages at Oldbury were fitted up as a Cottage Hospital which opened in 1865. So successful was this venture that it was proposed that a more permanent, purpose-built Rural Hospital should be provided and a committee was appointed to devise a scheme for that purpose. The members of the committee included Major Surman, Alderman, from Tredington; Mr Yorke, M.P., of Forthampton; Dr Devreux and Mr Sergeant. At the Annual Meeting in 1871, the Governors reported that an advantageous site had been purchased and that a design of "unpretending character" had been supplied by an eminent architect from Cheltenham, Mr Middleton. His plans were slightly modified by the committee but approval was given for work to start as soon as specifications had been received.

Following a service in the Abbey, five hundred people gathered to witness the laying of the foundation stone by Major Surman on 31st November 1871. The official opening took place on 31st July 1872, again after an impressive Abbey service at which the Bishop of Gloucester preached. Mr W. G. Healing declared the hospital open and in his address he extolled the merits of the architect and the great skills he had displayed. Further praise was showered upon the architect at the celebratory luncheon in the Town Hall, when it was agreed that, "The building is another of Mr Middleton's triumphs." The health of the builder and the architect was proposed after which both responded appropriately.

The red brick of the Gothic style building is relieved with blue brick string courses and Bath stone dressings and mullions. The hospital stood back from the road and when opened on 31st July 1872 was quite an outstanding building in this part of the town. It was shut off from the road by a substantial brick wall with dwarf palisading and was approached by two handsome gates provided by Collins and Cullis, the builders. Internally the hospital provided wards, operating room, surgery, dispensary, outpatients, mortuary and bathrooms. The wing beyond the windows immediately to the right of the entrance was added in 1880 and the hospital was further enlarged in 1892. Middleton's building is still easily recognisable and nowadays it provides sheltered accommodation for the elderly.

It might be appropriate at this point to say a few words about the firm of Collins and Cullis, builders, whom Middleton used both in Gloucestershire and in many out-of-county contracts. Thomas Collins was a Tewkesbury man, who was born and bred and lived in the town all his life. As a young man he was apprenticed to a stonemason.

He went into business on his own in 1841 and by the late 1850s he went into partnership with another local builder, William Cullis. They traded under the name of Collins and Cullis until the mid 1870s when Mr Cullis moved away from the town. The firm's archive at Gloucestershire Record Office contains many references to work completed for Middleton and his successors.

As one leaves Tewkesbury on the A38 for Malvern and Worcester, one passes on the left the Severn Trent Water Company's premises at The Mythe. An Act of Parliament in 1865 had authorised the Cheltenham Waterworks Company to extract water from the River Severn. In 1869 the Company purchased between five and six acres of the Brick Kiln Meadow on the south side of the eastern approach to the Mythe Bridge and work began on the construction of a permanent Waterworks. The plans provided for a pumping station with a Gothic style engine and boiler house and engine man's residence. "The style is pleasing and will be carried out in red and black bricks and Bath stone dressings." Although no reference is made to John Middleton in any of the press reports, his hand is clearly distinguishable in the design of the house to which L. W. Barnard refers in '*Ninety Years Past*' as having been designed by Middleton. At the time of construction Middleton was on the Sewerage Committee and The Water Supply Committee of the Cheltenham Improvement Commissioners and this may well have secured the contract for him. Although the Company's engineer is referred to in the proceedings of the stone laying ceremony, Middleton's work may well have been on terms similar to those for the Stockton and Darlington Railway in the 1840s, where the engineer drew up the requirements of the project and Middleton designed and planned the actual building.

Fig. 64 The Mythe Waterworks, Tewkesbury

If one looks at the front elevation of the engine and pump rooms and the engineman's house-minus the left bay extension-one cannot but be struck by the similarity in design to the house in Cheltenham's Wellington Square, named Eastholme and referred to in a previous chapter. The brickwork is the same, red with bands of purple brick and alternating red and purple voussoirs above the porch door and all the windows. Apart from an extra single light window to the right of the porch, the pattern for all the other windows at the front of the house is identical. The three gables too are identical as are the bargeboards, and apart from the absence of steps leading up to the porch which are unnecessary at the Mythe, the two buildings are almost mirror images each of the other. Completion was just after the start of the Middleton-Goodman partnership but designs would have been drawn well in advance of this. However as with most of Middleton's pre 1868 work, the archives for this particular project cannot be located.

Two further projects with which Middleton was involved in the Tewkesbury area are totally different in size and importance. Beckford Priory and Hall is on the Cheltenham to Evesham Road and was acquired by the Ashton Case family in 1883. The Hall was first occupied by Captain Henry Ashton Case, a convert to Roman Catholicism, in 1884 on his return from India. He added two wings to the property, one of which contained a chapel. The archives of the Middleton Practice contain accounts and plans for the work undertaken at Beckford and Middleton made a joint visit to the Hall with Captain Henry in 1883. The contract for decoration, additions, alterations and maintenance was awarded to Messrs Collins of Tewkesbury but not all the work was completed during Middleton's lifetime. He was able to supervise the building of the new tower and balcony, carriage sheds and stables, engine house, greenhouse and drainage, but the work on the two new wings was not completed until March 1887 two years after his death. This was under the supervision of his son, John Henry and his partners Prothero and Phillott. However all the plans for the new wings, which include the chapel and sacristy, are signed J Middleton FRIBA which his son John Henry never was. Some years later the firm also restored the medieval Catholic Chapel at Postlip, near Winchcombe, for the Forster family.

Work on St Giles' Church at Bredon, also near Tewkesbury, is included in the Middleton ledgers but there are no drawings to support these entries. The ledgers of Messrs Collins and Cullis of Tewkesbury also include references to the work on St Giles, for Middleton and Goodman, but it has not been possible to determine the extent of that work. An indication only is given when Collins and Cullis informed Middleton that they had inspected the spire of the church and found it "collapsed ten feet from the top" and this they agreed to repair for £100. Nine months later they wrote to Middleton agreeing to restore the spire "in accordance with your plans and specifications" for £85 with an additional £12 if the restoration of an additional seven feet was required. No further correspondence or accounts have come to light as is so often the case with the early work of the Middleton and Goodman partnership.

Sources consulted:
The Tewkesbury Advertiser November 1867. **Walton Cardiff Church.**
GRA, P349 VE/21; CW/1; M1/1.
GA, D1406.
GA, D843 4/1.
GA, P343 CW 3/1 **Twyning**.
GA, D2970 3/7.
Armstrong, B.E: *A Short History and Guide to St Mary Magdalene's Church, Twyning*. 1979.
GA, D2970 3/1. D2970/223..
GA, D2970 1/62; 3/1 **Forthampton**.
*The Tewkesbury Advertiser and Gazette*18.12.1869.
GA, D843 4/1.
Glynne, Sir Stephen: *Gloucestershire Church Notes*. 1871.
The Cheltenham Examiner 8th September 1871 and 15th October 1873. **Woolstone** Church.
GA, D2970 2/2; 3/1; 3/9.
GA, D843 4/1 p158.
Guide to St Martin de Tours Church, Woolstone. Church pamphlet. n.d.
Glynne, Sir Stephen: *Gloucestershire Church Notes*. 1871.
GA, P211.
Temple, Alexander: *Woolstone, Gloucestershire*.. c1906.
Gloucestershire Notes and Queries, Vol V **Leigh** Church.
GA, D22970 1/94; 3/7; 3/9, No 30.
GA, P199 CW 3/1-3.
The Tewkesbury Register and Gazette, 11th February 1865. **Tewkesbury Hospital**.
The Tewkesbury Advertiser and Gazette 2nd December 1871 and 3rd March 1872.
GA, D843 4/1. D2970 /194;TBR D8/1.
Barnard, L. W. *Ninety Years Past*. 1949. The **Mythe.**
The Cheltenham Examiner 2nd April 1869.
The Tewkesbury Register 12th June 1869.
GA, D2970 3.2;3/7; 3/9 No 19; **Beckford.**
GA, D2970 1/11.
Gloucester and North Avon Catholic History Society Journal Vol VIII.
GA, D843 p147 and 169**. Bredon Church.**
Willavoys, David. *'Thomas Collins' in Tewkesbury Historical Society Bulletin,* 1999.

CHAPTER XV

Berkeley Castle and smaller local contracts

The ledgers and contract books for the Middleton Practice naturally contain references to projects which are relatively minor. They also contain references to projects for which there is no evidence in the drawings portfolio, to designs for projects which were not accepted or for work which no longer exists. In many such instances, the Cheltenham or Gloucester press provides insufficient information about the work in hand or work completed but in most cases, it does at least give the name of the architect.

October 1882 saw the completion of work at Berkeley Castle for Lord and Lady Fitzhardinge, and although the Castle archivist was unable to trace any archive material, *The Cheltenham Examiner* and *Gloucestershire Notes and Queries* were ecstatic in their reports of the work and showered praise upon John Middleton for the skill and expertise which he had displayed. Middleton had been invited to make an assessment of work necessary for the restoration and repair of the Castle Chapel. This is the room now known as the morning room which was converted to such in 1923. The chapel dated from the fifteenth century and the roof beams and ribs were covered with scripture texts believed to be by the Biblical translator, John Trevisa, Vicar of Berkeley. The ends of the oak beams supporting the roof had become decayed and the whole structure was in a very dangerous condition. Middleton resisted the temptation to dismantle and destroy these timbers and thus preserved them for future generations. Instead he stripped the exterior of the roof of all its lead, and fixed strong beams strengthened with boiler plates above the roof. The actual roof was then suspended from these beams with wrought iron stirrups. The boarding for the new lead covering rested on this and the parapet hid any trace of the work being seen from below.

This work is undoubtedly the same work that is referred to in the ledgers under 'alterations' and repair of the Private Chapel, for Lady Berkeley,' as here again, reference is made to the repair and improvement of the chapel roof, but additional work is recorded comprising alterations to the chapel screen, flooring and furnishings; a new lectern; new altar hangings and new gas pendants. It is also accepted, although it does not appear in the GRO archives, that Middleton was responsible for the reredos behind the High Altar in the Parish Church of St Mary the Virgin.

The chapel work was a major undertaking and it is puzzling that it was not more widely reported in the press or architectural journals.

Of the smaller contracts which Middleton secured, the building of a new school at Brookthorpe, just outside Gloucester, is of interest because there is a considerable archive for the work which was begun in 1872, although Middleton had been first consulted in 1868. Correspondence between Middleton and the Rector of the parish shows Middleton's amusing forgetfulness. Having prepared all the plans, he had to write to the Rector to ask whether toilets were to be provided for boys and girls or just boys. "I forgot to ask – is it mixed or what?" Nevertheless Middleton's application to detail is quite astonishing in such a small contract and compares favourably with his specifications for the Hatherley Lane School in Cheltenham. "All visible woodwork is to have three coats of best varnish after having been well stopped, cleansed, sandpapered and twice sized." The school opened on Whit Monday 1874 and an initial School Inspector's Report commented most favourably on the excellent provision made by the architect.

Some contracts sound grand on paper but in effect comprised ordinary run-of-the-mill work, although some were for wealthy and influential Cheltenham clients. Among these can be mentioned the erection of a conservatory at Beauthornes in Hatherley Road, for William Watson in 1880, and the building of a servants' hall for Mr Edward Gillilan at Francis Close's former home, The Grange, in Malvern Road. However the sale particulars of the house in 1903 include reference to "A housekeeper's room or servants' hall," not quite the grand extension that the original contract wording might imply. Similarly in 1878 Middleton was asked to design the restoration and enlargement of the Imperial Coffee Tavern in the High Street, financed by Mr Gillilan. This was to encourage wage earners – the working class - "to prefer such establishments to the public house." *The Cheltenham Examiner* provided a lengthy report of the work upon completion, and praised "the expertise of Mr Middleton who has designed the facility," which in effect amounted to the construction of one large room to the rear of the existing building.

Several Cheltenham projects for which Middleton was responsible came about as a result of social or professional contacts. Sydney Lodge in Western Road occupied an enormous site between what is now St Hilda's and Malvern Road. Since at least 1864 the house had been the home of the Reverend R. H. Cooke, but he also provided accommodation there for nineteen College boarders and five domestic staff. Middleton's work included alterations and an extension and was completed by 1868. Its educational connections were continued after the sale of the house in 1892, when it was purchased as a boarding house by the Ladies' College. When the College sold it sometime around 1914, they transferred the students to the former home of Baron de Ferrieres on Bayshill and took the 'Sydney Lodge' name with them. The Western Road property was then renamed, but has since been demolished.

Further small or sometimes unidentifiable contracts included a house at Shurdington for a Mrs Leigh, a new east window at Pill Church in 1877, "alterations to the school for Colonel Noel" and a granite monument for the late Mr Morris. More mundane works are included in the small contracts section of the ledgers such as work on the drains at Roderick House, Suffolk Square; repairs and alterations at Alba Villa, Tivoli; and preparing plans and designs for additions and alterations to Leckhampton

Court for Mr Hargreaves in 1877; arranging the lease on Sandford House for G. M. Jackson and completing the subsequent repairs and internal decorations; alterations and additions to Hatherley Hall, Hatherley Road for General Wilkins and preparing plans and specifications for repairs, decoration and furniture design for Dr Havilland at 6, Bayshill Villa; alterations and additions to the Art Gallery at Nubie House overlooking Westall Green and planning and superintending the erection of the entrance gates at Arle Court for Mr W. J. Butt, at a cost of £1057, in 1876. The Lodge in Montpellier Gardens has often been ascribed to Middleton but in fact, although he did submit designs, they were rejected and those of J. Moore of Gloucester were accepted, in 1876.

Perhaps the most unusual and smallest of all his contracts was for the design and erection in 1879 of dwarf iron railings to surround the monument erected in Cheltenham Cemetery to the memory of the Reverend Dr. Morton Brown, who had been minister of Cheltenham Congregational Church since 1843. Dr Morton Brown had served with Middleton on several committees and they had become close friends. The monument still stands in a prominent position in the cemetery but the railings have been removed. Middleton was also responsible for erecting the memorial tablet to Mr Morton Brown inside the original Congregational Church in Winchcombe Street. This memorial was re-erected in the present Highbury Congregational Church when Dr Morton Brown's Church was demolished.

There are many other entries in the Practice's account and contract books but with less detail than those given above, making them impossible to identify. In other cases, one can only assume that entries refer to possible work that was not carried out or for which accounts plans and specifications are no longer available.

It is now appropriate in the following chapter, to look at some of the out-of-county work with which Middleton was involved and we will begin in Herefordshire.

Sources consulted:

Gloucestershire Notes and Queries Vol II p283. **Berkeley Castle.**

The Cheltenham Examiner 18th October 1882.

Correspondence with the Castle archivist has not revealed any references to this contract.

GA, D2970 2/2; 3/7.

Verey, David and Brooks, Alan: *The Buildings of England*, The Vale and the Forest of Dean.

GA, P64 SC5and SC21. **Brookthorpe School.**

GA, Middleton drawings and plans D2970/1.

GA, D2970 2/2; 3/1.

Kelly's Directory, Gloucester. 1896.

GA, D2970 3/7; 3/9; for **minor contracts.**

GA, CBR C5/6/1/1/1 Register of New Buildings.

The Cheltenham Examiner 19th October 1877, **Imperial Coffee Tavern.**

GA, D4858 2/1/1 1892. **Sydney Lodge.**

GA, D2970 3/9 entry No 6.

Gloucestershire Notes and Queries Vol III p581.

GA, D2970 3/1. **Arle Court.**

GA, D4335/57. **Montpellier Lodge.**

The Cheltenham Examiner 23rd July 1879. Memorial for **Dr Morton Brown.**

GA, D2970 3/1.

CHAPTER XVI

Work in Herefordshire

In addition to work in Gloucestershire, Middleton prepared plans and designs for clients in Wales, which we shall look at later, and in other areas in England. Not all of the projects are well documented and there is uncertainty about some of them, but the ones which illustrate the scope of Middleton's portfolio will receive appropriate attention.

North-west of Hereford lies the large village of Pembridge and a mile or so outside this village is Byletts, an estate which is featured in *Mansions and Manors of Hereford.* Middleton appears to have been involved as architect for the estate from the late 1860s when he drew plans of the old mansion and made a report on the estate, with a list of all the reusable materials, for the restoration and additions to Byletts, for the Court of Chancery. The reusable materials included all the beams and oak panelling valued at £180. Between 1870 and 1875 Middleton or his partner, Mr Goodman, made many visits to Byletts. Without entering the house one cannot fully appreciate the extent of Middleton's work but the similarity between Byletts and the work he did on Stardens in Newent is striking.

Fig. 65 Byletts

The house is built of orange brick with stone and brick decorative bands at the front. The main house, which seems to have been an irregular Elizabethan mansion rich in oak beams and oak panelling, is of three storeys apart from a gabled wing to the right which is of two storeys. It would appear from Middleton's plans that he added this wing to what was a quite small and plain house. Apart from the domestic offices, the ground floor originally comprised only a dining room to the right and a morning room to the left with bedrooms and attic space above. There were then no projecting bays to the front of the house. Middleton prepared at least twenty plans and a study of these show the extent of his work. He introduced the projecting porch rising through three storeys at the front of the house, he added the wing terminating in a steep gable to the right of the house, and on the ground floor he added a large drawing room, with delicate stone traceried windows on three sides. Behind this room he provided a study, a butler's room and a lavatory. Above these he added a dressing room, a boudoir lighted by an oriel window, and a bedroom. The heavy tall chimneystacks on the new wing are distinctive features of Middleton's work. In the grounds Middleton designed two estate cottages to the left of the main house, a lodge at the entrance to the estate, since demolished and a large greenhouse. The house, when visited by the author in 2002 had retained most of the features which would make it instantly recognisable as the work of John Middleton.

Middleton probably came by this contract through his association with the Cheltenham members of the Evans family which owned the estate and several of whom died in Cheltenham and were buried at Leckhampton. John Bowle Evans was a member of the Council of Cheltenham Ladies' College at the same time as Middleton was and he was also married to the daughter of one of Middleton's closest associates in the town, Charles Lloyd Harford of Evesham House, Cheltenham. Middleton also carried out work for John Bowle Evans at his home in Lansdown Place, Cheltenham. The Cheltenham Evans family still owned Byletts in 1913 but by then had leased it to Major General Sir Elliott Wood KCB.

Still in Herefordshire, and just north-west of Ledbury is Canon Frome Court. The estate in Middleton's day had been in the Hopton family for over three hundred years, although the present house dates from 1835. John Hopton inherited the estate on the death of his father in 1870 and employed Middleton to prepare plans for additions and alterations. However these were not extensive and simply included the erection of a billiard room, two bedrooms, servants rooms built over the offices in the east wing, and the present pillared stone porch to the north entrance. After WWII the property became a school and Middleton's billiard room became the school's music room. Today, Canon Frome Court has been converted into private apartments.

The only other domestic work in Herefordshire seems to have been for Christopher-Robert Lighton, J.P., Deputy Lieutenant of the county. He inherited Brockhampton Court near Ross-on-Wye from his father in 1875 and two years later engaged Middleton to prepare plans for enlarging the house. He did this by extending the property to the west of the main porch entrance and the extent of his work is clearly visible today in the different use of stone and the Bath stone dressings. One of his familiar date shields on the principal chimney-breast at the front of the house bears the date 1879.

Further enlargement was undertaken c1893 by the architect, F. Armitage of Manchester. Although there is little archival material available, an external tour of the property accompanied by the few drawings which do exist would convince the reader that *Pevsner* is indeed correct in identifying this Brockhampton House as the one on which Middleton worked.

The only known contract for ecclesiastical work in Herefordshire is for that at Staunton-on-Wye on the Gloucestershire-Herefordshire border. Middleton's visits began in 1877 and plans were prepared and signed Middleton and Son but no further details exist. However in *Littlebury's Directory* we find a reference to 1878 when "the spire was recovered with red Broseley tiles and a new south porch was added, by Middleton and Son of Cheltenham."

Sources consulted:
Herefordshire Record Office D32, *Historical Antiquities of Herefordshire*. **Byletts.**
Robinson, C: *Mansions and Manors of Herefordshire*. 1872.
Kelly's Directory for Herefordshire 1913. The date given there is rather later than the archives suggest.
GA, D2970 1/21; 2/2; 3/1; 3/7; 3/9.
Cheltenham Looker On. June 27th 1908 p7.
Kelly's Directory of Worcestershire, Herefordshire and Shropshire 1905 and 1913.
Littlebury's Herefordshire Directory.
Bowle Evans Memorials in Pembridge Parish Church.
Conversation with occupants in 2000 and a visit to the house.
The Cheltenham Examiner 29th February 1906.
Mansions and Manors of Herefordshire op cit. **Canon Frome Court.**
GA, D843 p366.
GA, D2970 2/2; 3/1.
Historical Antiquities of Herefordshire op cit.
Listed Building Description, 18.11.52. Grade II.
Kelly's Directory 1905.
Conversation with the widow of the last school caretaker, during a visit to the Court.
Burke's Peerage. The Lightons of **Brockhampton Court.**
Mansions and Manors of Herefordshire, op cit.
The Blue Guide Herefordshire.
GA, D2970 1/19: 2/2; 3/1.
Information supplied by the Manager on a visit to the property in 2002.
GA, D2970 1/186; 2/2; 3/1. **Staunton-on-Wye.**

CHAPTER XVII

Coleshill Park, Warwickshire

The town of Coleshill is the scene for Middleton's only known works in Warwickshire. Here there are two examples - one is by far the largest of any of his domestic designs and the other is the local school.

Coleshill Park is an estate which passed to the Digby family in the 1400s. At a later date, King James I granted the family the Sherborne (Castle) estate in Dorset and gradually the family spent more time there than it did at Coleshill. By 1786, Coleshill was described as "the deserted seat of the Digbys." The last of the Digby family died in 1856 and the estate passed through marriage to relatives named Wingfield who were granted the Digby name and Arms by Royal Licence, thus giving birth to the line of Wingfield Digby owners of the estate. By this time the manor had been so neglected that it was described as "long demolished" so that when Middleton became involved in the late 1860s nothing of the original house remained.

Why Middleton was consulted it is not at all clear, but by 1868 he had drawn plans for a new Coleshill Park mansion, plans which were to be considerably altered as work

Fig. 66 Coleshill

progressed. Between 1868 and 1874 Middleton and/or Goodman attended many meetings with Captain Digby either in Birmingham or Coleshill and eventually contracts were signed with the building contractors, Messrs Collins and Cullis of Tewkesbury. Work began in earnest in 1871 and the mansion was almost complete by 1873. The estate papers which are today lodged at Sherborne Castle in Dorset, include the very detailed building costs and accounts for all aspects of the work even to paperhanging and furnishings by Debenham and Freebody of Cheltenham. The contract, certainly the largest undertaken by the Middleton practice, produced an extensive red brick Tudor Gothic mansion with polychrome decoration under a steeply pitched roof.

The main entrance was by means of an impressive porte-cochere and to the left of this was an extensive service wing. The main hall was large, square and light, surmounted by a lantern roof and a grand arch led to the stairway. The ground floor rooms still contain many of the original features of the house – panelled wooden ceilings, masses of stone carvings which decorate the stone walls, carved stone ceiling bosses, heavy wooden and mechanically controlled window blinds and carved stone fireplaces. One can still see in the dining room a buffet recess identical in design to the one at Westholme and similar to that at Eastholme, two houses designed by Middleton in Cheltenham.

Two flights of stairs lead to the first floor's square, open gallery, from which doors lead to various rooms and passages. Entry to the tower was gained from the gallery through an archway filled in with a wood and glass screen, which bears a striking similarity to that on the first floor of the original main entrance to Cheltenham Ladies' College. One room in the tower has an ecclesiastical feel and contains a large gothic arched recess which is deeply and heavily carved. The window recess is a patchwork of delicate carving on the walls on either side of the window and is another superb example of the stone carver's art.

Next to the house are the remains of extensive coach house and carriage blocks and beyond these an enormous walled garden. Middleton must have wondered whether he would ever see completion of this vast undertaking which, although not an exceptionally attractive building, does not deserve the rather dismissive comments to be found in a 1925 history of Coleshill and its Parish Church: "The house, though handsome, well appointed and Elizabethan in style, is only Victorian in age and therefore does not call for further description." The total cost of the work was just under £14,000 which was an enormous sum by today's standards.

The Wingfield Digby family occupied the mansion until about 1910 at which point it became an Anglican Diocesan retreat house, and much later, a hospital. After a considerable period of neglect, the estate has been sold to developers who started work in 2002, promising to preserve as many of the original features as possible.

At the same time as Middleton was supervising the construction of the mansion, he was also preparing drawings for an elementary boys' school in the town. This was to be known as Back Lane School. The project was financed by Captain Digby's father who was Vicar of Coleshill. The school was built of red brick with blue brick patterns and white stone dressings. The roof was steeply pitched and had miniature dormers. One of the gables on the school bears a roundel containing the emblem of the Digby family. In a walled garden adjacent to the school Middleton designed the Headmaster's house on the side of which there is still the date shield for 1872. A doorway in the high brick garden wall gave access to the school grounds. The school closed in 1982 and the property was on the market in 2001 for £495,000.

Sources consulted:

Pennant, Thomas: *Perambulations of Warwickshire.* n.d.**Coleshill Park**

GA, D2970 1/54; 3/1; 4/31.

GRA, D843 4/1.

Kelly's Directory, 1892.

Coleshill and Its Parish Church 1925.

Tyack, Geoff: *Country Houses of Warwickshire.* 1989.

Hayfield, C. & Watkins, A: *Coleshill and the Digbys.* 1995.

March, Rosemary: *Sherborne Castle.* 1985.

Sherborne Castle Estate Archives. Mrs Ann Smith, Curator and Archivist.

I am much indebted to Mr Stuart Briddick of Messrs Peter Hing and Jones, Birmingham, who was working on conversion plans for Coleshill. He accompanied me on a tour of the property, provided valuable information and shared with me his photographic archive of the property at the time of his initial inspection.

GA, D2970 1/39; 4/1 **Coleshill School.**

G. R. Darby & Co Ltd. Coleshill Estate Agents.

CHAPTER XVIII

Here and there

Just over the county boundary from Gloucestershire into Wiltshire is the straggling village of Brinkworth near to Wootton Bassett. Middleton was first consulted in 1871when he reported that the Parish Church there was in a dreadful condition with the side walls leaning fourteen inches out of perpendicular, the roof entirely decayed and the flooring virtually gone. Once Middleton had secured the contract, the chancel was dismantled, the stones being numbered piece by piece and later reused. A new roof of panelled oak with carvings at the intersections was prepared and the floor was re-laid with Minton tiles. Coloured glass was placed in the east window at the expense of the incumbent, the Reverend Mr. de Quatteville and his brothers and sisters in memory of their parents. New seating for the nave and chancel was also provided. While scraping whitewash from a wall near the chancel, some wall paintings were discovered and a complete painted figure on a pier near to the nave was also revealed. The work had been completed "in accordance with the designs of Messrs Middleton and Son" by November 1879.

Turning away from Gloucestershire and its surrounding counties we discover that there were some private contracts that Middleton accepted in the London area too, but his son John Henry may well have supervised some of these. A contract in the early 1870s, which was probably the result of a personal recommendation, was for the enlargement and repairs to a house, number 26, James Street, Buckingham Gate, London. The client was an M.P., Mr Arthur Pendarves Vivian, who was married to the daughter of the third Earl of Dunraven. At the time of the contract being signed, the Vivians were living at number 19 in the same street. The work on the house and stables amounted to just under £4,000, about seventy-five times that in today's terms. The work included new oak ceilings and ornamental plastering, refurbishing of some of the rooms, the provision of domestic offices, stabling and a laundry. Middleton made over thirty visits to Mr Vivian but being a member of the Hanover Club, Hanover Square, he no doubt stayed there overnight. An interesting connection between this contract and Cheltenham lies in the fact that Middleton bought on Mr Vivian's behalf, some old oak carving from Arle Court, Cheltenham and this was conveyed to Vivian's new house in London. Sadly, St James Street which was very near to Buckingham Palace, no longer exists.

Middleton was also responsible for work at St Peter's Church, Eaton Square, possibly through the recommendation of Dorothea Beale who was a close friend of the incumbent, the Reverend Mr. Wilkinson, who later became Primus of the Scottish

Episcopal Church. Unfortunately all parish archives were destroyed during World War II and no details of the work survives.

However, still near to London, work which again is sparsely documented, was completed at Hampton Court House dating from c1765. The house is very near to Hampton Court Palace and in 1872 Middleton was responsible for designing a Picture Gallery, conservatory and orangery. The work was completed by 1875 when Middleton and Goodman received their commission on the three phases of the work which had amounted to just under £9,000. In 2004 the house was a private school but the orangery still stands intact and attached to one side of the property.

Two contracts of considerable interest date from c1879 and are not at all related. That furthest away from Cheltenham was for the church at Sowerby, near Halifax. The Church of St Peter was built in 1766 and consecrated in 1847. The nave has two rows of Corinthian columns which compulsively lead one's eyes to the apsidal east end. In 1878 Middleton was awarded the contract for "the erection of a new organ chamber and vestry, re-pewing, and the making of certain other alterations." This work was more aesthetic than structural and included some furnishings, designed by John Henry. Eight visits were made to the church from Cheltenham and various parcels of sample materials and designs were posted from Cheltenham between July and August 1878. Plans for the alterations, re-pewing and furnishing designs are held by Gloucestershire Archives and at Wakefield and all are signed 'Middleton and Son.' *The Cheltenham Examiner* carried a comprehensive report of the work and focused especially on the alterations to the chancel, carried out by Martyn and Emms of Cheltenham. The work was done in Serpentine Mexican and Irish marble and leading to the altar is a tessellated pavement. Behind the altar the apse is decorated with Jacobean oak panelling into which has been inserted an oak credence. There is much Italian stucco-work above the panelling. The old box pews were replaced with free unappropriated sittings apart from those in the gallery. "The whole is of a classical character and the work shows great care and attention," was the local press's summary of Middleton's work.

Fig. 67 Sowerby, St Peter's Church

John Henry's work certainly consists of an altar frontal, seven feet four inches in length and designed in silk and gold on best Lyons velvet, and a brass and iron lectern which is most ornate and carries foliage and bunches of grapes. The ornate but somewhat heavy pulpit is also to his design. It must be admitted that there is a strong similarity between the work in the chancel and that designed by John Henry at Christ

Church, Cheltenham and one can be forgiven for suspecting that perhaps John Middleton junior had far more influence over the work at Sowerby than the archives and publicity gave him credit for.

The same may be true for the church at Dinnington, north of Newcastle-upon-Tyne. Middleton designed a new church for the town in 1883 but the plans, signed J Middleton, FRIBA, bear the inscription 'Woolsington Church.' The confusion arises because the benefactor of the new church was a Captain, later Major, Henry Bell of Woolsington, just three miles distant from Dinnington. Major Bell had married Helen, the daughter of Sir William Burdett Bt. of Cheltenham and the church contains several memorials which give clues to his Cheltenham connection. The Major, who was a respected and knowledgeable archaeologist, was living with his wife Helen, in Cheltenham, at Chalfont Lodge, The Park, when Middleton arrived in the town. He was elected Churchwarden of St Philip's Church in 1863 and he was later a member of the Friends in Council to which Middleton also belonged. On the death of his brother, Capt Bell inherited the paternal estates in Cumberland and moved there with his wife. She died in 1878 after which Captain Bell devoted his life to improving the estate and the lot of the estate tenants. He also built the new church at Dinnington, employing John Middleton as architect. Middleton died before Dinnington Church was completed but the contract was continued by his son, John Henry, who made some slight alterations to his father's plans, resulting in the building we can see today. These later designs for Dinnington Church are signed Middleton, Prothero and Phillott and appear to be c1885. The completion certificate was issued in November 1886.

It has been seen necessary to devote a considerable space to work beyond the boundaries of Gloucestershire but there is surely much more yet to be discovered. The same is true of his work in Wales, where some of his contributions have only recently been identified. It is this part of his career that we will now consider.

Sources consulted:

The Builder 4th October 1879. **Brinkworth Church.**

GA, D2970 1/17; 2/2; 3/7.

Tour of the church.

GA, D2970 3/1. **Mr A. P. Vivian, M.P.**

GA, D843 4/1.

Correspondence about the **Hanover Club** in the Maenclochog, Pembrokeshire, file - see chapter XXIV.

GA, D2970 3/9 No 11. **Hampton Court House.**

Visit to the school, and correspondence with the owners 2002.

West Yorkshire Archive Service, Wakefield Headquarters re **Sowerby Church**.

GA, D2970 1/227; 3/1.

The Cheltenham Examiner 19th March 1879.

Correspondence with the Incumbent and a visit to the church in2002.

GA, D2970 1/55. **Woolsington Church.**

GA, D2970 3/7; 3/9. **Dinnington Church.**

CHAPTER XIX

An Introduction To Wales

During Middleton's residence in Cheltenham, he made frequent excursions into Wales and was responsible for the restoration and rebuilding of several ancient churches, and the design of some new ones. Many Welsh churches had suffered from neglect in the years leading up to the 1840s and many of the parishes covered extremely large and thinly populated areas. Fundraising was a major challenge as so many of these parishes served very poor members of the community and although, thanks to the enthusiasm and commitment of the Bishops, parishioners were keen to renovate or restore their place of worship, there was often a long delay between the initiation of the project and its actual completion. Grants were available from organisations such as the Incorporated Church Building Society (ICBS), but the very high standards they demanded often meant that applications for grants were turned down – and in many instances, not even applied for.

Of nearly two hundred drawings and plans in the Middleton archive, about a third are for projects in Wales and it may well be that his friendship with the Dowager Countess Dunraven of Clearwell was to a large extent, the reason for his services being engaged. He also built up a firm and lasting friendship from 1874 until his death, with the Bishop of St David's, the Right Reverend Basil Jones, who had strong Cheltenham family connections. Most of Middleton's work was in the counties of Cardigan, Carmarthen and Pembroke and although this could have presented travel difficulties in so far as supervision of projects was concerned, it must be remembered that train links with the Principality were extremely efficient at the time. One could leave Cheltenham at 6.10 a.m. and arrive in Swansea by 11.35, or Carmarthen by 12.58. If preferred, one could leave Cheltenham just after midnight and reach Carmarthen by 6 a.m. On arrival Middleton could guarantee that his client would have arranged transport to the site of the work for which he had been engaged and we know from his correspondence that overnight accommodation was never a problem. Middleton frequently enjoyed the hospitality of his Welsh clients, as he was accustomed to do at Clearwell.

It has already been shown that many of Middleton's contracts came about through personal recommendation and the three examples of his domestic work in Wales which we shall consider in this chapter, fall into that category. The two most significant are near Newcastle Emlyn in Cardiganshire.

There were of course many other projects for which Middleton submitted designs, some recorded, some legend. Through lack of funds, unsuitability of design, change of incumbent or in some cases, Middleton's death before the plans had been approved, several projects were not completed. Some are worth mentioning however, as they provide further evidence of the vast amount of work with which he was engaged in Wales and the many different challenges which he addressed.

Middleton must have become very familiar with the roads and lanes of Wales, especially in Carmarthenshire and Cardiganshire and to some extent in Pembrokeshire. His ledgers and log books carry frequent references to travel expenses to these places including overnight accommodation, and this is especially true for the late 1870s up to his death in 1885.

CHAPTER XX

The Houses of Bronwydd and Mount Gernos

Mount Gernos had long been the seat of the Parry family and was inherited through marriage by Gwinnett Tyler who married Judith Parry. The house, dating from c1800, was situated above the ancient house on the estate named simply Gernos. Middleton's association with Captain Tyler probably began as a result of the marriage of Tyler's sister into the Dunraven family of Clearwell, in the Forest of Dean.

Between 1869 and 1877 Middleton's office books contain many references to expenses on account of Captain Tyler and these range from the cost of sending telegrams, to cab fares, rail fares and preparing plans and specifications for work at Mount Gernos. Middleton had been called upon to remodel the house and this he did with great effect. Externally he enlarged the south-west garden front by the addition of two large, two-storey square projecting bays with a conservatory between. He closed up the main entrance in the south-west front and opened up a new main entrance in the rear north-east portion of the house. Around this he created a porte-cochere be-

Fig. 68 Mount Gernos

tween the northern and eastern bays. On the north-west façade he added another two-storey projecting bay and further windows were inserted into the south-west elevation.

Internally, several rooms were remodelled to create domestic facilities and more accommodation. Most of the woodwork was in true Middleton taste – 1870s gothic. The wooden staircase which was built especially for the Tylers, was of stained pitch pine and replaced an earlier one of oak. Stonework throughout was very skilfully worked, much of it in Bath stone, and displayed a profusion of carved floral designs, fruit, and musical instruments. These all bear a striking resemblance to Middleton's designs for Coleshill Park in Warwickshire and Holy Apostles' Church in Cheltenham, on both of which he was working at the same time as he was engaged at Mount Gernos.

Published evaluations of Middleton's work on the house seem to agree that it had been spoiled externally by Middleton's additions and alterations. The house passed out of the family's hands c1920 and was allowed to deteriorate. Today, the only proof of its existence is to be found in the two stone bays of the south-west front which stand ghostlike as though surveying the valley below. Nearby, protected by industrial sheeting, lie piles of carved stone samples that once graced the ground floor rooms of Middleton's remodelled home for Gwinnett and Judith Tyler. A lodge to the estate was also designed by Middleton and, unlike its parent house, it is still intact today.

Middleton's contract books also contain entries over a twelve months period, for the erection of a mill at Gernos. There was quite a thriving woollen industry in the Teifi Valley in the 1880s and although a mill may already have existed at Maesllyn,

Fig. 69 Maesllyn Mill

Fig. 70 Llangynllo. St Cynllo's Church

Gwinnett Tyler engaged Middleton to build the present structure using the Yorkshire pattern of a large weaving hall with the roof supported by pillars. In 2001 only the shell of the building remained and plans were being considered for its conversion into holiday accommodation.

Middleton's earliest known work in Wales was the rebuilding of the Tylers' Parish Church of St Cynllo at Llangynllo in Cardiganshire. The plans are signed and dated John Middleton, Architect, 1867. The medieval church was in a pitiful state of disrepair and it was decided to demolish the church apart from the tower, "which will provide a link with the past." The church stands about four miles north of Newcastle Emlyn overlooking the estate of Bronwydd, now a ruin, but formerly the home of Sir Thomas Davies Lloyd, Bart, 1820-1877. It was mainly though his support and that of his near neighbour, Mr. Gwinnett Tyler of Mount Gernos, that agreement was reached to complete the work on St Cynllo's. As this is undoubtedly Middleton's most tasteful and successful works in Wales, it deserves a fuller description than that which has been accorded his other works.

The church is built of stone in the Early English style and consists of nave, chancel and vestry with the south porch beneath the tower and spire. On the north side is the organ chamber beneath which is the boiler house. All the windows and door arches have carved stops on each side, mostly of crowned heads, but some bearing mitres. There is a fine, small, rose window above the west window matched by one above the east window. Internally, the church is an excellent example of High Victorian architecture and proudly displays the influence of the Cambridge Camden Society. The windows are of Bath stone and the rest of the decoration boasts many examples of marble and stone from Cornwall, Devon, California and Italy. The detail and beauty of the stone carvings are breathtaking and are the work of R. L. Boulton of Cheltenham with whom Middleton worked on many projects in Gloucestershire and Wales. *Evan Davies* writing in 1905, says with reference to St Cynllo's that "It is difficult to imagine anything more beautiful than (Boulton's) carvings of the angels."

Fig. 71 Llangynllo. St Cynllo's Church

I am greatly indebted to *Brian Whatmore* for permission to make use of his excellent description of St Cynllo's which he produced in 1998. This enabled me to interpret more profitably on my visit to the church, the vast amount of rich ornamentation that the church contains. The nave is lined with red brick and bands of black brick. The roof is open and supported by six arched principals resting on twelve carved stone corbels, each carved with flowers, foliage–roses, shamrock, thistle, oak, acorns, wheat, grapes, geraniums, willow, violets, lilies, daisies–and a harp! Between the corbels the walls are decorated with strong polychrome patterns. The nave floor is tiled and patterned and the walls carry several ornate, large memorials to the Lloyd family. Some of these are of white marble and alabaster, some decorated with ornamental canopies, coloured coats of arms, urns, cypress and alabaster and black marble mouldings. There are also several brass memorial tablets. The nave pews are of pine and several still support the original three-branched candelabras, similar examples of which are also to be seen at Clearwell.

The chancel arch is deeply moulded. Two short columns of Italian marble support this arch, each column resting on a superbly carved group of three angels carrying scrolls. These bear the legend, "Glory to God in the Highest, on Earth Peace, Goodwill Towards Men." On either side of the chancel are the carved heads of the four Evangelists, Mark and Matthew facing the west end and Luke and John looking towards the altar. The chancel walls are lined with Bath stone, relieved with bands of red stone. The floor is laid with Minton encaustic tiles. The choir stalls carry interesting brass candelabras. The chancel roof is canted and divided into beautifully decorated panels separated by richly decorated mouldings. The panels themselves are strikingly similar to those used in Middleton's home in Cheltenham. The roof is supported by eight carved angels of delicate design and according to *Whatmore* they are adaptations from the well

Fig. 72 Llangynllo. St Cynllo's Church

known painting by Fra Angelico. Each of the angels is in a symbolic attitude of prayer, and praise, and playing a musical instrument. The two over the sanctuary have their hands folded in an attitude of perfect contentment.

The original vestry designed by Middleton is now the organ chamber the arch to which is supported by further groups of carved angels carrying musical instruments and bearing scrolls with the legend, "O Come Let us Sing Unto the Lord". The sanctuary is separated from the chancel by an open brass altar rail, and within it is an intricately carved credence and alongside it a sedilia supported on a national emblem—a bunch of leeks.

Beneath the east window is a richly carved and diapered reredos in which is placed a vesica of alabaster containing a floriated white marble cross with five coloured marble bosses. On either side of the vesica are roundels containing carved figures of worshipping angels. This reredos was presented to the church by Rosa Tyler of Mount Gernos and the central cross was the personal gift of John Middleton.

The font near the south door was given "In memory of Grace Beatrice Daisy Tyler, April 25th 1869" her baptism day. It is octagonal and made of Caen stone with a red granite base. Clusters of water lilies support the bowl whose eight sides are deeply sculptured, four with emblems of the evangelists, and between them the other faces bear scenes connected with the theme of baptism, including Christ's baptism. The pulpit is richly ornamented with eight varieties of stone. The upper section of variegated alabaster rests on a dais of Caen stone. The walls of this dais carry carved stone figures of St Paul, St Peter and St John the Evangelist. Each figure is separated by pillars of Italian marble above which are medallions bearing the carved heads of St David and St Cynllo. This pulpit was presented to the church in memory of George Marteine Lloyd, 1830-1849.

A further memorial of interest is a statue of the Old Testament character, Ruth, which stands in a superbly carved stone niche opposite the pulpit. The statue was given by Sir Thomas Lloyd in memory of his wife who died in 1871. *Whatmore* says that Ruth was probably chosen as being considered less 'high church' than the Virgin Mary would have been in the 1870s.

Family vaults of the houses of Bronwydd (Lloyd) and Mount Gernos (Tyler) are in the graveyard at the west end of the church and Middleton was involved in their design.

The cost of building the church at Llangynllo was in the region of £2,200 but restoration in the 1990s saw an urgent appeal to the tune of £80,000.

Thomas Lloyd inherited the Bronwydd Estate from his father in 1845 and was himself created a baronet in 1863. During the early 1850s he built as his residence the Gothic style castellated mansion, which overlooked the Teifi Valley, and is now nothing more than a ruined shell. Francis Jones in his *Historic Cardiganshire Homes and their Families* informs us that Sir Thomas made a gift to Llangynllo Church of one of only two jewelled sets of plate in Cardiganshire. The oaken chest which contains the plate was made from an oak beam from the old church of Llangynllo. Placed inside this chest is a vellum scroll, carefully mounted, which reads: "To the honour and glory of God. The plate for Holy Communion was presented to Llangynllo church by the House of Bronwydd and Mount Gernos, AD 1870."

It is worth recording here that in the Middleton archive at Gloucestershire Archives, there is reference to plans for an additional room at Newport Castle in Pembrokeshire, another property belonging to the Lloyd Family of Bronwydd. These plans included examining and reporting on the round tower which was to be converted into rooms for the new Corporation; 'superintendence and monument to the late Lady Lloyd, and designs for bookcases, screens, doorways etc in the entrance hall at Bronwydd, paid 1878.'

Presumably the monument to Lady Lloyd refers to the statue of Ruth in Llangynllo church but it has not been possible at the time of publication to provide evidence that Middleton actually completed the other works. This might provide a fascinating opportunity for further research by a Pembrokeshire local historian.

An undertaking similar to that at Llangynllo was accepted by Middleton in 1877 for the thirteenth century parish church at Newport, Pembrokeshire. The newly appointed Rector in 1875 described the church as disfigured and dilapidated. Two years later a more detailed report described the rotten window frames, leaking whitewashed roof, and walls so cracked that ivy was flourishing inside the building. Middleton had by this time earned a considerable reputation and respect in the Principality and his acquaintance with the Lloyd family of Bronwydd may have been influential in securing for him the contract for the total restoration of this large and ancient building.

The Middleton archives contain very detailed accounts of the work and all sorts of indemnity clauses and time scales are carefully worded. The work was to be completed in stages and each stage had to be approved on completion before the next stage could proceed. Middleton's drawings and specifications are very detailed from the size of bolts to the thickness of each piece of wood carving and the minute details on the window carvings.

While the work was in progress – this time with full support from the ICBS – Middleton found several medieval features which had hitherto been hidden. He also based some of his restoration work in the south transept on the details contained in an old 1810 print which he had come across. The total restoration included raising the height of the nave walls and replacing the ceiling; rebuilding the chancel to a longer and lower design; replacing the wooden windows with stone ones; removing the old gallery from the back of the church and inserting a vestry under the tower and replacing all the old furnishings, apart from the Norman font which he restored. At the opening service of the newly restored church, the Bishop of St David's commented, "Mr Middleton's restoration has provided one of the handsomest and most commodious churches in Pembrokeshire." Local craftsmen had been employed wherever possible but all the ironwork was provided by the Cheltenham firm of Letheren. *Mr. F. G. Wallace-Hadrill* writing in 1989 commented that Middleton had produced a good solid church, "with none of the polished marble and Gothic fantasies of his work in Cheltenham, and in avoiding such excesses, had produced a fine handsome church."

Sources consulted:

Tyler family information from *The Landed Gentry of Great Britain* and *Historic Cardiganshire Homes and their Families.*

Parkinson, A. J. (4.2.1981) Crown Copyright: Royal Commission on the Ancient and Historical Monuments of Wales.1981, ***Gernos.***

Davies, Evan, *Hanes Plwyf Llangynllo.*

GA D2970 1/202; 2/2; 3/7.

Cadw 1985.

L Baker-Jones, *Princelings, Privileges and Powers.*

The Teifi Store.1980-81.

Orbach, Julian: correspondence with author.

Lloyd, Thomas: *The Lost Houses of Wales* and correspondence with the author.

GA D2970 1/108; 3/1; 3/7. **Llangynllo.**

Whatmore, Brian, *A Guide to St Cynllo's Church, Llangynllo,* and correspondence with the author.

Correspondence with Mrs. I. Flint and Mr. M. Jefferies of St Cynllo's Church.

Horsfall-Turner, E. R., *Walks and Wanderings in County Cardigan.*1902.

Davies, Evan, op cit.

Appeal Literature 1999.

The Welshman, 1st April 1887.

An Architectural Study; ***Newport Castle.*** 1992. Crown Copyright: Royal Commission on the Ancient and Historical Monuments of Wales.

Visit and conversation with Mr. and Mrs. Holt, Newport Castle, 2002.

Pembrokeshire Record Office HPR/33/47: HPR/33/48; **Newport Church**

GA, D2970 1/132; 2/2; 3/7.

The Welshman 3rd October 1879.

Wallace-Hadrill, F. G: *The Parish Church of St Mary, Newport, Pembrokeshire.*

John Middleton, an Englishman in Wales. St Mary's Newport, Parish Magazine 1992;

Hurlock, Richard: correspondence with author.

CHAPTER XXI

Churches along the Teifi Valley between Cardigan and Lampeter

Besides the churches at Llangynllo, Llandyfriog and Lampter, which are mentioned elsewhere in this precis of Middleton's work in Wales, there are at least eight other churches associated with Middleton strung along the Teifi Valley. In this chapter we will visit them all beginning with Llechryd and moving up the valley towards Llanybydder in the east.

During the 1870s work was undertaken at Llechryd where old was completely replaced with new. The church dedicated to St Tydfil must look today very much as Middleton designed it. The bell tower above the west window still houses its bell, and the south porch of wood, stone and partial glazing is exactly as he designed it. Internally the church is of painted brick and the windows are not coloured. Around the walls of the raised chancel runs a band of terra cotta laurel leaves in relief, which is the only ornamentation visible. The pews are of red pine. This is definitely not one of Middleton's most sumptuous churches as the completion accounts suggest - £1,083 paid in 1880. However, at the consecration by the Bishop of St David's on 13th September 1878, the church was packed "with the elite of the district," and in the evening over three hundred people were reported to have crammed into the building for the litany.

Fig. 73 Lechryd . St Tydfil's Church

A rather poignant reminder of Middleton's work at this period is to be found at Llandygwydd where he had been invited to design and in-stall a new reredos and pulpit in 1874. The reredos "of most chaste and beautiful character," was given in memory of a Mrs Buck. The base was of Bath stone with diaper pattern, supporting nine arcades flanked by larger outer ones containing the commandments carved, and coloured in gold, on white marble. The arches of the arcade were supported by beautifully polished granite shafts with floriated capitals. The central arch contained a cross of white marble set on an engraved black marble background while the outer arches had white alabaster medallions featuring grapes and corn. A pulpit donated in memory of William Bradstock for whose widow Middleton had worked previously at Cenarth, was also richly engraved and enriched with alabaster medallions, all with gold floral patterns. The bookrest on the pulpit was of polished marble. Sadly, the church was demolished in 2000 and all that now remains is the floor, and the font standing isolated at the west end and totally exposed to the elements. Unfortunately the author has not been able to trace any pictorial representation of Middleton's reredos and pulpit.

Fig. 74 Llandygwydd Church, the remains

Middleton and Goodman's next contract after Llangynllo was for the rebuilding of St Llawddog's Church at Cenarth, situated on an eminence above the village and the River Teifi. It appears that Middleton decided to completely demolish the seriously dilapidated church and as this was being done, ancient tombs were discovered under the foundations suggesting an even earlier Christian site. The rebuilding was one of those projects where work was completed in stages as funds became available. Although the foundation stone was laid in October 1868, the church was not formally opened until 1872 having cost £1,700 but Middleton's account books for 1885 recorded that the account had not yet been settled – "A/c rendered – bad debt." *The Welshman* made special reference to the elaborately carved chancel arch, the beautiful circular window at the west end and the Hardman glass in the apse. Questions were raised however about the weathering suita-

Fig. 75 Cenarth, St Llawddog's Church

Fig. 76 Henllan, St David's Church

bility of the Bath stone which had been used. The font is perhaps the most interesting feature in the church. Its bowl, which Middleton mounted on an elaborate stone marble pedestal, dates from c1100. Middleton's designs for Cenarth have received some criticism. The *Carmarthenshire Antiquary 1973* described it as too ostentatious and recent appeal literature quoted one architect who said that the only good thing about the church was its ceiling.

The 1880s saw the building of a new chancel at St David's Church, Henllan for the Reverend J. Powell. This was completed by April 1882 and at the opening so many people attended that the service had to be 'relayed' outside. *The Cardigan and Tivyside Advertiser* for May 1882, spoke of a bazaar that had taken place ten months previously to raise funds so that now a beautiful new chancel had been added to the old structure which had been renewed and was a credit to both architect and builders. This little church is situated in an isolated spot near to the river.

Fig. 77 Clydey, St Clydai's Church

Reference has already been made to contracts which were completed in stages, as funds became available. It was also often the case that architects drew up plans for a project that was not actually started until some years later and St Clydai's church at Clydey is one such example. The church dates from c1490. Repairs had been carried out in the early 1800s but in 1874 Middleton was invited to inspect the church with a view to carrying out a complete restoration. A contemporary visitor to the church described the church as being "of the rudest type, built of common rubble masonry with a modern deal roof, no ceiling and having no features of any merit." Further visits by Middleton took place between 1875 and 1877.

Fig. 78 Llandysul, St Tysul's Church

The ICBS objected to Middleton's initial plans and engaged the architect R. K. Penson to inspect the building and provide a written report. Once again, as at Llanfihangel Ystrad, the local incumbent was determined to proceed with the rebuilding whatever the outcome of Penson's report and when the ICBS refused to consider a grant for Middleton's designs, an appeal was launched to raise funds by public subscription. Work began in earnest in 1878 and amounted to rebuilding the church, replacing the battlements on the tower and adding a small spire–which was removed in 1973. The opening service was not held until July 1889 however, four years after Middleton's death. This delay is due to the fact that Middleton was not the only architect involved in the project. He was responsible for the first stage, the nave and main body of the church. The chancel was designed later by D. Davies of Llandysul, after Middleton's death, although it had been provided for in the original drawings.

Llandysul like most of the places that have been described so far in this chapter, stands on the banks of the River Teifi. The church of St Tysul dates from the thirteenth to fifteenth centuries and is of unusual design. It has a nave, chancel, two side aisles and a square tower, but no transepts. Its size placed a tremendous financial burden upon the parishioners but Middleton and Goodman were invited to prepare plans for the church's restoration in 1872. Internally the church was plastered and whitewashed and in true Middleton fashion, he removed the plaster to reveal the original stonework. He raised the nave roof so that it was higher than that in the aisles and the chancel was completely rebuilt and heightened. Here again, carved stone musical angels bear witness to the craftsmanship of the firm of R. L. Boulton of Cheltenham, as does the carved pulpit. In effect the church was almost totally rebuilt, only the tower escaping Middleton's attention.

Fig. 79 Llandysul, St Tysul's Church (source unknown)

Nearby is Capel Dewi, rebuilt in 1835 as a chapel-of-ease to Llandysul. Middleton was invited to prepare designs for alterations

Fig. 80 Capel Dewi, St David's Church

to the church in 1883. He made drawings for its enlargement, together with alteration and restoration of the windows, the chancel arch, the roof, tower and nave. Work did not start until June 1884 and was completed after his death in 1885. On entering the church one cannot but be impressed by the fine single, open barrel roof, plastered walls and moulded arches to the transepts. The chancel arch was not restored but there are segmented pointed inner arches to the chancel windows. This was a considerable contract in terms of costs and it is sad that Middleton did not see it completed.

Ledger entries contain references to work on several buildings for which there is little actual documentary or visual evidence and these include a new vicarage at Capel Dewi.

In 1878 a complete rebuilding of the church at Llanybydder was first promoted by Colonel and Mrs H. Davies Evans of Highmead. This did not receive an immediate response. It would seem that Middleton was well and truly out of favour with the ICBS at this period. In 1884-1885 the ICBS reported that only the tower and lower walls were worth retaining. Middleton's plans were considered pretentious and unsuitable, the Perpendicular style was considered inappropriate and the chancel arch was out of place. Even the buttresses were considered 'bad.' Middleton therefore submitted amended plans showing amongst other details, new tracery, a new chancel arch, a vestry on the north side and a new porch. *The Welshman*'s report of the opening in October 1885 praised the early geometrical style which Middleton had used throughout the restoration. Interior furnishings were replaced and new tiled floors laid. The roof was renewed as were all the windows. Even the tower received attention, and was

Fig. 81 Llanbydder Church

given a new concrete roof on iron joists. Only the vestry and the turrets on the tower had had to be deferred until a later date due to lack of funds. The whole project took just over a year and "now the church is one of the neatest in the neighbourhood." *The Welshman* ended its report by paying tribute to the architect, "the late John Middleton of Cheltenham whose too laborious life ended suddenly in the present year."

Sources consulted:

Tivyside Advertiser 29th December 1876; 13th July 1877 and 13th & 27th September 1878, **Lechryd Church.**

GA D2970 3/1. **Llandygwydd.**

The Welshman 27th February 1874.

GA, D2970 1/25; 2/2; 3/1. **Cenarth Church.**

Listed Building Description, Reg No. 14226. Grade II.

Lloyd, Thomas, correspondence with author.

St Llawddog's Church, Cenarth, leaflet available in the church. n.d.

Thomas, C. Mervyn: *Cenarth Falls, Cenarth-Wales.*

The Tivyside Advertiser 21st June 1872.

The Carmarthenshire Antiquary: Transactions 1974.

GA D2970 1/72; 2/2; 3/7. **Henllan.**

The Tivyside Advertiser 12th May 1882.

The Carmarthenshire Journal 22nd September 1882.

GA, D2970 1/36; 2/2; 3/1 and 3/7, **Clydey Church**.

Brash, Richard Holt, quoted in *St Clydai Church History and Guide.* Tony Law 1993.

ICBS file 7960.

The Welshman and Pembrokeshire Guardian, July 1889.

GA, D2970 1/100; 2/2; **Llandysul.**

Cadw ref 22/D/16/(5) Grade II*.

The Tivyside Advertiser 12th June 1874.

St Tysul's Church, Llandysul, Parish History 1978.

Listed Building description Reg No 10,574.

GA, D2970 3/9 **Capel Dewi.**

The Welshman 11th April 1883.

Cadw 22/D/27(6).

Listed Building description, Reg No 10,585 Grade II.

ICBS file 8879, **Llanbydder**.

GA, D2970 3/9.

The Welshman, October 30th 1885.

Hurlock, Richard, correspondence with author.

CHAPTER XXII

St David's College, Lampeter

The most significant of the 'transitional' work, i.e. work begun by Middleton senior and completed by Middleton junior, must surely be for the new accommodation block and lecture rooms at St David's College, Lampeter. This was started by the father c1884 and completed by the son, in 1887.

The Council of St David's College realised in 1884 that there was a need for more accommodation at the College. Plans were prepared, and the foundation stone of the new building was laid in 1885 by the Archbishop of Canterbury the Most Reverend and Right Honourable Edward Benson – hence the name, The Canterbury Building. The project did not take long to complete. The opening took place on 24th June 1887, and the ceremony was performed by the College Visitor, the Bishop of St David's the Right Reverend Basil Jones. Part of the bishop's speech referred to Professor Middleton

Fig. 82 Lampeter. The Canterbury Building

- meaning John Henry - and those who had worked with him on the building. Later he referred to "my friend the architect, Mr Middleton." The exterior of the building did not excite much enthusiasm however. *The Cambrian News* felt that it impressed one "more with an idea of utility than ornamentation," although this was probably as a result of a shortage of funds rather than a lack of imagination.

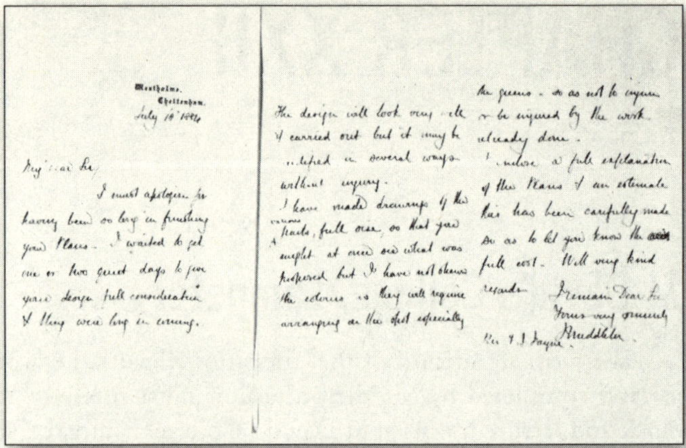

Westholme.
Cheltenham.
July 14 1884

My dear Sir,

I must apologise for having been so long in finishing your Plans. I waited to get one or two quiet days to give your design full consideration & they were long in coming.

The design will look very well if carried out but it may be [illegible] in several ways without injury.

I have made drawings of the various parts, full size, so that you might at once see what was proposed but I have not shown the colours as they will require arranging on the spot especially the [illegible] so as not to injure or be injured by the work already done.

I enclose a full explanation of the Plans & an estimate this has been carefully made so as to let you know the full cost. With very kind regards

I remain Dear Sir
Yours very sincerely
J Middleton

Rev. F. J. Jayne.

Fig. 83 John Middleton's letter re The Canterbury Building, Lampeter

In the College archives, there are several letters which indicate that the original plans were prepared by John Middleton senior. He was familiar with the town, having undertaken minor repairs to Lampeter Church in 1872 and in 1884 he had drawn plans for additional rooms for Lampeter Schools, another project completed after his death. He also tendered, unsuccessfully, for the reordering and redecoration of the College Chapel in 1884 and it was at this time that his plans for the Canterbury Building were drawn. These plans were modified slightly after his death by one of his partners, Henry Prothero, but were not acceptable to the College Council. Several alternative proposals were made during the next few months and by September 1885 Middleton junior took over the supervision of the contract and all future correspondence to do with The Canterbury Building is signed J. Hen. Middleton. The completed building bore only slight resemblance to the design submitted by Prothero and John Henry Middleton would appear to have adapted his father's original design of a stone building with Llandewi stone facings.

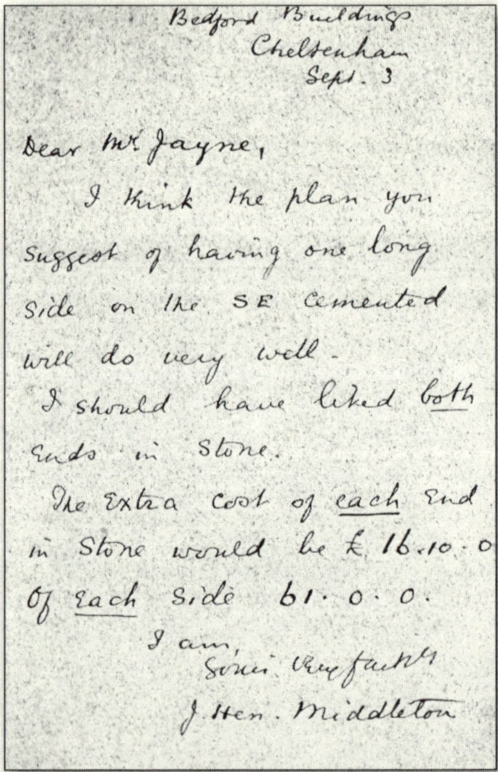

Bedford Buildings
Cheltenham
Sept. 3

Dear Mr Jayne,

I think the plan you suggest of having one long side on the SE cemented will do very well.

I should have liked both ends in stone.

The extra cost of each End in Stone would be £ 16.10.0
Of Each Side 61.0.0.

I am,
Yours very faithfully
J. Hen. Middleton

Fig. 84 John Henry Middleton's letter re The Canterbury Building

It was quite an impressive building for its size, but due to poor foundations, it became unsafe and was demolished in 1971. Some of the original interior beams painted with arms and crests have been restored and are to be reused on the College Campus. The foundation stone is in the entrance to a new building on the same site as the Canterbury Building, but with different geographical alignment.

Sources consulted:

GA, D2970 1/86; 3/1.

History of ***St David's University College.*** University of Wales Press, Vol. I 1977

The Architect 14th August 1885.

St David's College Archives H/4/4; H/7; H/7/4; H/7/43.

The Cheltenham Examiner 21st October 1885.

The Cambrian News July 1st 1887.

A Bold Beginning, University of Wales, Lampeter; Glimpses of an Unfolding Vision 1827-2002. Various contributors.

Listed Building description, **St Peter's Church**. Reg No 10,430. Grade II.

CHAPTER XXIII

From the Aeron Valley to Aberystwyth

Fig. 85 Llanfihangel Ystrad, St Michael's Church

A double project which lasted from 1873 to 1883 was undertaken for Captain Herbert Vaughan at Llanfihangel Ystrad. Middleton visited the ancient and dilapidated medieval parish church of St Michael in 1873 and was invited to submit plans for complete restoration. However his plans were again, not to the liking of the ICBS who described them as exceedingly bad, "so bad that it is suggested that the whole scheme be reconsidered." Middleton's response was along the lines that his survey drawings of the original church had been mistaken for his new design. In his opinion the old church had no redeeming features – wooden windows, very rough – even hideous arcading and no mouldings. Middleton also added that the bellcote was in a dangerous condition and that whatever happened, he, (Middleton), Captain Vaughan and the Rector intended to proceed with a complete rebuilding. This was in effect completed by 1877 at a cost of £1,300 and a report ten years later said that he had left nothing of the original except a font dating from c1180, an old oak chest dated 1661 and some medieval masonry in the aisle and nave. The Vaughans were not a wealthy family and

Fig. 86 Llanfihangel Ystrad, St Michael's Church

Fig. 87 Aberaeron, Holy Trinity

one is prompted to ask how so much money was raised for the project without any ICBS assistance? However the proposed tower and spire did not materialise and the porch and bellcote are additions of 1928.

The other project in the parish mentioned earlier, was in connection with the vicarage. On completion of the work on St Michael's, Middleton was asked to report on the condition of the Old Manor House, for the Church Commissioners. His drawings of the building, plans and specifications for an almost total restoration amounted to £1,074, paid in full in January 1885. This contract would seem to have referred not to Vaughan's Manor House, Brynog, but to the 18th century Llanfihangel vicarage, the Old House, which was on the same site as the present vicarage, but a little further to the north and nearer to the road.

Holy Trinity Church in Aberaeron is a seaside church where work was again completed in stages. A Georgian style preaching house had been built in 1838 to cater for the needs of an influx of English or Anglicised minor gentry who had settled in the town when the new harbour was being constructed. By 1870 it was considered too dangerous for worship. Middleton first visited the town in 1871 – staying overnight in a hotel at a cost of £3.16.4, and decided that a new church was the only solution. His designs provided for a building in the French-Gothic style, with seating for four hundred persons. Work soon got under way and the first part to be completed was opened in 1872. This consisted of a five bay aisle-less nave and south-east chapel. The roof design, the pulpit carving and the arcading in the nave resting on marble columns, merited much praise in contemporary accounts of the opening. The consecration took place in August 1875, but everyone doubted whether the architect's plans for a tower and spire would ever be realised. However, determination on the part of the congregation

Fig. 88 Llandeiniol, St Deiniol's Church

Fig. 89 Aberystwyth, Holy Trinity Church

bore fruit and work was completed in 1880. Since that date, there has been a major change to Middleton's apsidal east end, the present square one having been erected in 1900. In 2002 major restoration work was undertaken but externally, the church looks very much as Middleton designed it.

A very pretty 1830s church at Llanddeiniol, a few miles south of Aberystwyth, was restored and enlarged by Middleton in 1882/3. The chancel was rebuilt entirely from the foundations and an apsidal sanctuary was provided. The resulting effect completely transformed what had been a very simple church.

However, the largest and most northern of Middleton's Welsh work is to be seen at Aberystwyth itself, where he was commissioned to design a new church. As fate would have it this is another example of a church designed by Middleton senior and completed by his son, John Henry. The architect's perspective, preserved in the church, identifies the "New Church, Aberystwyth. Middleton and Son, Architects." Underneath is written in much smaller script, "Now Prothero, Phillott and Barnard, Cheltenham." The origins of the church bear striking resemblance to the origin of Cheltenham's Delancey Hospital. Each began in the mind of a wealthy benefactress whose families contested the bequests. In the case of the church at Aberystwyth, the matter was taken to Court by the Rector of Henllan who was one of the Trustees. In 1872, the Court upheld the wishes of the benefactress, Miss Morice, with the proviso that only £500 be spent towards erecting the church, the residue being used to provide for its endowment. It is for this reason that the church was built in stages, as and when fund raising provided sufficient income. In fact, the whole project spanned the years 1881 through to 1899. Between 1881 and 1883 Middleton made eleven visits to the town. The first advertisement inviting tenders for the erection of the nave appeared in 1882, and the foundation stone was laid the following year. *The Cambrian News and Welsh Farmers' Gazette* described the ar-

Fig. 90 Aberystwyth, Holy Trinity Church

chitect's plan for the completed church – "a five bay nave, chancel and transepts with tower springing from the crossing. The nave is lofty and very large and light. On either side are five large traceried windows with two further windows at the west end all fitted with Cathedral tinted glass".

Fig. 91 Aberystwyth, Holy Trinity Church

Today, the east end is framed from the nave by the tall slender and graceful arches of the chancel and tower, which has been built only as far as the lower stages. This is a plain yet impressive building and one which deserves much more recognition than it receives, although its situation does not encourage the casual visitor.

Aberystwyth provided the setting for the final domestic contract which Middleton accepted in Wales, at the time that he was working on the nave of Holy Trinity Church. *The Builder* of 10th January 1885 reported the award of the contract and on 17th January, exactly one month before his death, *The Architect* carried an invitation to tender for a new house, 'Frongog, near Aberystwyth,' for Mr E. Jones. Tenders were to be delivered by 3rd February, to the architect John Middleton of Cheltenham. According to his office books, Middleton had visited the site in March 1884 and once plans had been drawn he estimated the cost of the contract at £2,795. Sadly, he did not live long enough to even see the start of the work which began in May 1885 and lasted until December 1887. Delay in completion may have been due to his sudden death and subsequent negotiations with his successors. Mr Jones himself did not live long enough to fully enjoy his new gentleman's residence for he too died only a year after moving in, in August 1888. He was a wealthy man, leaving estate valued at £23,010 and his tombstone records that he was a J. P., that he had a son and daughter and that he was one of the two original acting churchwardens of Holy Trinity Church.

Fig. 92 Aberystwyth, Frongog

Frongog is set in a prominent position overlooking vast open countryside. The exterior is rather austere with a three-bay asymmetrical front. The entrance is in the centre bay through a wooden door surrounded by a glazed screen. A small entrance hall leads into the main hall, where one is met by an elaborate and impressive dog-leg stairway turning from left to right with carved newels and balustrade. On one side of the stairway, at first and second floor levels, an open, stone, gothic-arched screen looks down into the hallway. Lighting the hallway is a glass lantern roof. Ground floor rooms have impressive fireplaces and cornicing. In the garden is a lovely ornate summer house which seems to be contemporary with the house itself. The grounds contain outbuildings added to the house by Mr Jones' widow in 1889 but by 1892, Mrs Jones had vacated Frongog, although she continued to live in Aberystwyth.

Fig. 93 Aberystwyth, Frongog

Sources consulted:
GA, D2970 1/106; 2/2; 3/1; **Llanfihangel Ystrad.**
ICBS file 7915. Information courtesy Thomas Lloyd.
The Welshman 19th June 1885.
Listed Building description. Reg No 17430. Grade II
Cadw: Welsh Historic Churches Project: *St Michael, Llanfihangel Ystrad.* c1998
GA, D2970 1/107 No 1.**Llanfihangel Vicarage**, the Old House; and D2970 3/1; 3/7.
GA, D2970 3/1, **Aberaeron Church.**
National Library of Wales, *Aberaeron* 22, 23, 26-29 and 30-33.
Carmarthenshire Journal 20th October 1871.
The Tivyside Advertiser 13th and 20th September 1872
The Welshman 4th October 1872.
Listed Building description Reg No 9,995 Grade II
The Tivyside Advertiser 13th September 1878.
Listed Building description Reg No 17,135 **Llanddeiniol**
GA, D2970 1/97; 3/7.
The Tivyside Advertiser 23rd November 1883.
Listed Building description Reg No 17,135. Grade II.
Carmarthenshire Journal 16th November 1883.
GA, D2970 1/2; 1/3; 3/9 No 24. **Aberystwyth Church Nave**. May 1883-May 1884.
Cambrian News and Welsh Farmers' Gazette, 13th August 1886.
National Library of Wales, 1883-1897; 19 plans and elevations.
Cadw 22/B/250(3).
Listed building description Reg No 10,145 Grade II.
Jones, Janet, *Holy Trinity Church, Aberystwyth, The First One Hundred Years.* 1986.
South Wales Directory. n.d.
Correspondence with Mrs Vi Davies, Aberystwyth.
GA, D29701/4; 3/2; 3/7; 3/9 No 22. **Frongog.**
The Builder January 10th 1885.
The Architect 17th January 1885.
Conversation with the owners and tour of the house and grounds, 2002, courtesy Mr. R. Feasey.

CHAPTER XXIV

Two Pembrokeshire Churches

There is little correspondence as such in the firm's archives and what little exists elsewhere is usually to be found amongst his clients' correspondence. The work Middleton completed in Pembrokeshire, on the old church at Maenclochog, provides a fascinating written account of the relationship between client and architect and I am grateful to *Pembrokeshire Record Office* at Haverfordwest for making it accessible to me.

St Mary's Church is in the centre of the village and since its eleventh century foundation it has been rebuilt or restored on several occasions. In the late 1870s the vicar sought diocesan advice about a suitable architect to undertake restoration work on the church and the Bishop of St David's replied, "I venture to suggest my friend Mr Middleton of Cheltenham who has done much good work in the Diocese." His suggestion was accepted and within a short while, the Bishop had written to the promoter of the project, the Honourable Mrs Margaret Owen, to inform her that Middleton was arriving at Bishop's Palace at Abergwili the following day and would be making a visit to Maenclochog to inspect the church. After Middleton's visit, the vicar wrote to Mrs Owen and from this correspondence we get a lovely picture of John Middleton, then aged sixty, whom the vicar described as "a nice old man." Middleton inspected the church, the vicar's 'boy' fetching a ladder for him, and then he departed for London where he was going to inspect another church. "I think he must be a man of great experience – I should have liked you to meet him... He liked the old church and said it was very clean... He said that I must restore all the chancel at my own expense as I am Rector of the living."

Middleton later wrote to Mrs Owen from his home, Westholme, in Cheltenham, informing her that his designs would be as simple as possible as she had requested. He insisted however, that the Rector "wishes to restore the chancel himself." He made certain observations about the building and its furnishings, including the front of the pulpit which he considered to be of Queen Anne vintage. This he wished to retain but alter somewhat as it looked too large for the church. He also admired the very old font which he said he would thoroughly clean and place on a plinth. The Bishop wrote to Mrs Owen saying how impressed he was with Middleton's observations but that there were two issues which he wished to discuss with the architect. Unfortunately the remainder of the letter is missing.

Middleton kept up quite a lengthy correspondence with Mrs Owen, supporting her efforts to raise funds through Bazaars and suggesting to her how many tenders she should consider and how to go about making a final decision. "I think from what I know of Welsh builders, five months will be required from the time of commencing. There is a good deal to do." It would seem that Mrs Owen also questioned his professional fees for he later wrote to her from Cheltenham, assuring her that his fees were those agreed by the RIBA "of which I am a Fellow." Some weeks later, Middleton was again in London, staying at the Hanover Club, and from there he wrote to Mrs Owen, congratulating her on having decided upon a contractor. He informed her that he was soon going to Mr Fitzwilliams at Cilgwyn, Newcastle Emlyn, and after that to eight other places including Maenclochog, taking about ten days in all. On his return to Cheltenham, Middleton sent her all his plans and drawings together with an acceptance of her kind invitation of hospitality. The plans were in the first instance, for the work which she was funding – excluding the chancel. The chancel plans followed in November 1880, "very simple but in keeping with the rest" and by June 1881, completion had been achieved. He referred to the previous week's official opening of the church, where everything had "gone off so satisfactorily," and assured her that she was quite correct in refusing to pay the contractor until he, Middleton, had signed the completion certificate. He stressed that any further problems must be referred directly to him.

The Welshman provided a comprehensive account of the work done: the old church was pulled down and the walls were re-used and newly pointed; new roof, new pews, new metal window frames, restored and repositioned memorial tablets, and a rebuilt chancel for which the Rector contributed £200. The Bishop included in his opening speech how pleased he was that it was he who had introduced his friend the architect to the Owens.

This project illustrates the vast amount of travelling and correspondence Middleton was involved with and the vast amount of time that he was away from home. The Bishop's comment above also illustrates how much of Middleton's work was the fruit of personal recommendation.

Before leaving Maenclochog, reference ought to be made to the vicarage. The fact that Middleton designed one , and even visited the proposed site, is beyond doubt, but it may well have been too ambitious a project for a poor parish at that time, in view of the cost of the church restoration.

Another Pembrokeshire project with which Middleton was involved was for the pre-Norman church of St Christiolus at Eglwyswrw. The decision to restore the church was taken in 1879 and work began in 1881. Middleton was of the opinion that the foundations on which he was to work were the original pre-Norman ones. His work amounted to a complete rebuild with the porch, the chancel arch of large proportions and the flanking buttresses being completely new additions. This was another case of accepted designs costing more than was readily available and although Middleton's fees were paid in part by January 1884, an account rendered for the balance was issued shortly after his death a year later.

Fig. 94 Eglwyswrw, St Christiolus' Church

Sources consulted:
Pembrokeshire Record Office, Haverfordwest. HPR 29/1. **Maenclochog** Archive.
GA, D2970 1/116.
GA, D2970, St Peter's Eaton Square, London. Correspondence with the incumbent 2002.
The Welshman 10th June 1881.
GA, D2970 3/7.
Carmarthenshire Journal, 8th June 1883. **St Cristioulus, Eglwyswrw.**
GA, D2970 1/57.
West Wales Historical Records Vol. I p293.
Listed Building description Reg. No 15,880.

CHAPTER XXV

Churches in the vicinity of Carmarthen

Fig. 95 Carmarthen, St David's Church

Middleton was no stranger to completing or revising work originally begun by R. K. Penson and this was certainly the case at St Clears. Penson had undertaken a partial restoration between 1853 and 1855 partly funded by private donations and partly by a grant from the ICBS. Middleton was called upon to complete the restoration and made nine visits to St Clears between 1881 and 1883. It must be stressed that his work was a continuation not an undoing of Penson's earlier work, apart that is, from Penson's chancel roof which he replaced. Surprisingly for Middleton, he did not interfere with the Norman chancel arch, perhaps regretting the unforgivable destruction he had allowed at Greatham in his pre-Cheltenham days. In fact, rather than destroy the past, Middleton revealed it in the discovery of an Early English chancel window which had been previously walled up. This he copied in the side windows of the chancel and imitated it in the three light east window. His work was described in *The Welshman* as "very tasteful."

Llanfihangel Abercywyn was inspected by Middleton in 1882, and he made drawings of the existing building, plans for its restoration and a drawing for a completely new church. Restoration was to cost about £800 and a new church would cost £1,000. In the event it seems that 1882 saw only the replacement of window tracery and the rebuilding of the bellcote.

Perhaps the most complicated of Middleton's contracts was that carried out at St David's Church in Carmarthen. The original church faced north-south and was opened in 1837. It was enlarged by R. K. Penson c1850 by the addition of a four bay nave to the west of the existing building and the re-erection of the north end sanctuary against the east wall. The former sanctuary became the organ chamber. Middleton was engaged

Fig. 96 Carmarthen, St David's Church

to redesign the chancel in 1884 as a memorial to the previous incumbent. This he did by extending the east wall into the churchyard and raising the chancel floor above that of the nave. A chancel arch, thirty two feet in height and supported on polished granite columns was also provided. Gothic style pews were installed in the chancel as was also a clergy stall of similar design. A new font and pulpit were created by local craftsman William Davies and a new altar was also installed. Again Middleton did not live to see his designs completed and the church was not consecrated until April 1886. The work had cost £1196. The local press described St David's, "formerly an ugly church, but now beautiful." *The Welshman* praised the architect – "We always expect beautiful work when Middleton and Son are employed."

The church of St Mary, Kidwelly was severely damaged by lightening in February 1884. The top twelve feet of the spire and twenty-five feet down one side were destroyed and a large part of the building was damaged by falling masonry. The north west of the nave roof was broken, the ancient font was totally destroyed and the west end gallery was totally demolished. On the advice of the Bishop of St David's Middleton was appointed architect of the restoration. By the end of May work had started on the spire, and by November work on repairing the nave was well under way. However the whole process of restoration was a lengthy one and was not completed until 1889, the year in which Middleton's son and partners rebuilt the chancel. The new font in the church was actually designed by Middleton's son, John Henry.

Fig. 97 Llanpumsaint, St Celynen

During 1882, the rebuilding and enlargement of the pre 15th century church of St Celynen at Llanpumsaint was completed. In contrast to many previous contracts this one seems to have been well financed. Middleton made good use of old materials and retained existing struc-

Fig. 98 Llansadwrn, St Sadwrn's Church

tures wherever possible. The alterations were in the traditional Early English style, so favoured by Middleton, with an extremely long chancel in comparison to the nave. The chancel arch is semi circular and of oak resting on handsome stone corbels. During the rebuilding, Middleton discovered a squint on the north side of the chancel, and used its shape to influence his design for the new chancel windows. An ancient holy water stoup was also preserved near the main door and a pre-reformation altar stone was brought into the church from the graveyard and placed under the new altar. A new pulpit was provided but the ancient font was retained. The Bishop remarked at the opening service in June 1882, "This is one of the most satisfactory restorations I have seen." The Press described it as one of the most beautiful little churches in the neighbourhood, but perhaps too small, holding just 90 people. This deficiency was addressed in 1892.

During the late 1880's a chapel-of-ease was provided by the Middleton practice at Capel y Groes near Llanllawddog just south of Llanpumsaint. Correspondence revealed that there was some disagreement between John Henry Middleton and the ICBS concerning the style of this chapel. The ICBS wanted a "medieval forgery", as Middleton called it, whereas he wanted a more contemporary nineteenth century style building. They criticised his attempt, as they saw it, to bring together "almost every style in a small building while none are well treated". He argued that the Society had often quarrelled with his late father too regarding taste. In his defence Ewan Christian said of John Henry Middleton that he was a very able architect but one who had dedicated himself to archaeology. After some amendments the plans were finally approved in 1886 and the chapel was consecrated in 1888. A Vicarage was also constructed by the practice in 1886.

Plans for the restoration of the medieval church at Llansadwrn, a small village north of Llandeilo, did not progress smoothly either. A design had been first prepared by Llandeilo architect John Harries in 1876 but this was considered "thoroughly bad in all details" by the ICBS and even the Bishop of St David's was not happy with it. Middleton was consulted in 1881/2 and prepared a full restoration programme, but again, the work was not completed until some months after his death in 1885. It would appear that, as with other similar projects, fund raising was a laborious challenge and three months after the work was completed the accounts had not been paid. In typical Middleton style, the plaster was stripped from the chancel to reveal the rubble stone, although the nave walls remained unstripped. A north wall door and west-end window were blocked in, and new pews, priest's stall and oak pulpit were provided, the total restoration cost amounting to £770.

Llansawel, another village north west of Llansadwrn, is an example where Middleton's restoration plans are dated 1879 but work did not start until six months after his death, when it was supervised by his son John Henry and his partners Messrs Prothero and Phillott. The roof was heightened, new gothic windows were inserted in the nave and at the east end, the chancel floor was retiled at great cost and the roof was panelled, new furnishings were provided throughout the church, a vestry was added to the building and gravestones in the churchyard were repaired.

Fig. 99 Llansawel, St Sawel's Church

Ledger entries contain references to work on several buildings for which there is little actual documentary or visual evidence. These include the erection of outbuildings at Abergwili, the episcopal residence of the Bishop of St David's, and alterations to the Palace itself; several small contracts in Cathedral Close at St David's including a new Chapter Lodge for the Dean and Chapter; and alterations and additions to the Vicarage at Abergwili for the Archdeacon. This vicarage had been designed by R. K. Penson c1855. Middleton's advertisement for tenders appeared in *The Welshman* on the day he died, 13th February 1885. In the event, the work was completed by his son.

Fig. 100 Llansawel, St Sawel's Church

Sources consulted:

ICBS file 8879

The Welshman 14th April 1882 and 11th July 1884. **St Clears.**

Listed Building description Reg. No 9,409, Grade II*

Listed Building description, Reg. No 25,485. **Llanfihangel Abercywyn**
GA, D2970 1/24 **Carmarthen, St David's Church.** St David's is facing serious structural problems in 2006 and will probably have to close.
GA, D2970 3/9 No 28.
Hughes, Clive, *A Brief History of St David's Church, Carmarthen.*
Correspondence with the Rev Clive Hughes.
The Welshman 3rd August 1883.
The Tivyside Advertiser, 30th May 1884, **Kidwelly** Church.
Carmarthenshire Journal 30th May 1884 and 12th September 1884.
Jones, D Daven, *History of Kidwelly* 1908.
Listed Building description, Reg. No 11,878.
GA, D2970 1/79.
Listed Buildings description Reg. No 9403 **Llanpumsaint**
Carmarthenshire Journal 15th April 1881.
The Welshman and The Carmarthenshire Journal, 2nd June 1882.
Kelly's Directory. 1896 and 1914.
The Welshman 4th February 1887.
GA, D2970 1/114; 3/7; 3/9, **Llansadwrn**
ICBS file 8003
Listed Building description, Reg. No 10,945.
The Welshman 23rd February 1883.
Carmarthenshire Journal 24th April 1885.
GA, D2970 1/112; 2/2; 3/7; 3/9 No 35, **Llansawel.**
Carmarthenshire Journal 24th August 1885.
Listed Building description Reg. No 10949.
Price, F:. *The History of Llansawel* 1898.
St David's Diocesan Gazette *Llansawel.* n.d.
The Carmarthenshire Antiquary Vol. IX 1973.
South Wales, Ancestral, Biographical and Pictorial. n.d.
GA, D2970 1/111; 3/7 **Llanllawddog Vicarage.**

CHAPTER XXVI

Cilgwyn

A domestic project, much grander than that at Mount Gernos, but in the same area and on completely different lines, was accepted by Middleton for the Fitzwilliams family. Part of the Cilgwyn Estate had been inherited by Edward Compton Lloyd Hall in 1849 but as a mark of protest at not having inherited the whole of the estate under the terms of his father's will, he assumed the old family name of Fitzwilliams. Edward's third son Charles Home Lloyd Fitzwilliams was born in 1843, married in 1869 and fathered eight sons and two daughters and he succeeded to his father's estate in 1880. Middleton had first been consulted in 1871 and he was involved with the family until his death in 1885.

Charles' parents lived in Adpar House on the estate and Charles and his family lived in the adjacent Emlyn Cottage, a delightful cottage ornee, built c1790 by John Nash. Charles was not over enthusiastic about Adpar House and when his father died in 1880 he had no intention of using it as a home. In fact he had the house demolished in 1910 as "not being fit for a gentleman to live in." At the time of his father's death, Charles was in the process of making considerable alterations to Emlyn Cottage by improving the water supply, rebuilding the kitchen wing and making substantial alterations to the accommodation itself. However while this work was being carried out, Middleton was again consulted about the possibility of building a new mansion with stables, farm buildings and gate lodges. A letter from Fitzwilliams' estate manager, Mr Robinson, and addressed to Mr. J. Middleton at 1, Bedford Buildings, Cheltenham, dated September 10th 1880, confirmed this intention. "I send you plans and sections of the field whereon it is intended to erect the new house etc. for Mr Fitzwilliams." Fitzwilliams' vision had in fact developed to such an extent that it called for the demolition of Nash's cottage ornee to make way for a larger, more impressive house on the site.

Fig. 101 Cilgwyn Mansion

Middleton's fees for preparing the various designs amounted to 5% of

Fig. 102 Cilgwyn Mansion, in 2004

the estimated cost of £3,800. Several visits were made to inspect the site between 1881 and 1883 and eventually tenders were invited in April of that year. Fitzwilliams also made one or two visits to Cheltenham to consult Middleton and work was soon underway. Emlyn Cottage was demolished and Fitzwilliams and his family moved in to Adpar House. Charles Fitzwilliams' diaries are held at the National Library of Wales at Aberystwyth, and entries for this period illustrate his interest in every aspect of work on the new mansion as it developed, displaying occasional annoyance at lack of progress. During site visits, Middleton stayed at Adpar House, having been collected from the station by Charles Fitzwilliams himself. On other occasions, when Middleton stayed at Mount Gernos with the Tylers, Fitzwilliams visited him there.

However all was not light and joy. Fitzwilliams kept a careful watch on work in hand and several letters exist in which he challenged Middleton quite sharply over costs, late delivery of materials, inconsistency on the part of the contractors in the interpretation of plans, and the design of some of the door furniture. At one point workmen had downed tools because they were awaiting instructions on how to progress with a certain stage of the building – Middleton was urged to send details "at once!"

The house that Middleton designed was an unattractive, grim, complex and heavy building in the shape of a hollow square, the open side being at the rear of the house. The front was of three bays with a central tower in which was placed the main entrance. Around the front and left side of the house ran a canopied veranda. Attached to the right side of the house was a conservatory above which was the date stone for 1885. To the rear of the house were stables and domestic offices with a clock and bell turret on the top of the kitchen wing. The huge staircase in the entrance hall came from the Great Exhibition in Paris of 1875 where it won a prize but it was incorrectly measured for Cilgwyn - people were constantly

Fig. 103 Llandyfriog, St Tyfriog's Church

Fig. 104 Llandyfriog School

tripping over it during dances. The author has not been able to gain access to the interior but when last he visited the property, the house was in very poor condition and had a sad, neglected appearance. In 2004 it was being advertised for sale.

A similar story to that at Kidwelly is to be found in the archives for St Dyfriog's Church at Llandyfriog, near Newcastle Emlyn. Middleton visited the church while working at the Fitzwilliam Mansion, Cilgwyn, and prepared several sets of plans for restoration in 1881 but he died before work could begin. After his death designs for a new church were prepared by Mr. H. Prothero, one of the partners in Middleton, Prothero and Phillott. The old church was demolished and the present one was consecrated in 1890. The churchyard contains several burial inscriptions to the Fitzwilliams family.

Middleton's design for the school at Llandyfriog was completed however and work began in April 1884. It was not one of Middleton's most straightforward projects as there were frequent problems with contractors over failure of materials to be delivered on time and minor differences of opinion between Middleton and the promoter of the scheme, Charles Fitzwilliams for whom Middleton was working on Cilgwyn Mansion. The school was eventually completed shortly after Middleton's death. Middleton obviously loved working in Wales and it is sad that it was while working at Cilgwyn that he was seized of a paralytic stroke from which he died.

Sources consulted

Gravestone details of **Edward Compton Lloyd Fitzwilliams**.

Charles Home Lloyd Fitzwilliams's obituary, *Tivyside Advertiser* 15th May 1925.

Correspondence with Thomas Lloyd.

Suggett, Richard, *John Nash, Architect in Wales.*

GA, 2970 1/99; 3/7and 3/9.

National Library of Wales, **Cilgwyn Estate Records Group (II) 72**, Diaries of Charles H Ll Fitzwilliams..

Correspondence and conversation with Mr K Jones of Newcastle Emlyn.

Mr E. Fitzwilliams of Old Cilgwyn for photographs of the house and family.

Jones, F. *Historic Cardinganshire Houses and Their Families.*

Correspondence with Helen Palmer, *Ceredigion Education and Community Services Department.*

The Welshman, 13th April 1883.

Listed Building description, **St Tyfriog's Church**, Llandyfriog, Reg. No 10,739, Grade II

CHAPTER XXVII

John Middleton, Obituary

The Gloucestershire Echo of Friday 13th February 1885 carried the following announcement:

> We regret to announce the death of Mr. Middleton the local architect of Cheltenham, well known as the designer of some of the principal buildings in this town chiefly those of the ecclesiastical type, of which All Saints may be mentioned as an example. On Saturday Mr. Middleton was in Wales where he was seized of a paralytic stroke, and he died this morning at 7 o' clock.

The Cheltenham Examiner was somewhat more sensitive and warmer in its report of John Middleton's death and more comprehensive in its record of his accomplishments when it made this announcement on 18th February:

> With unfeigned regret we record the death on Friday last, after a very brief illness, of Mr. J. Middleton, a gentleman whose name has been for many years widely known as an architect and the impress of whose skills is written on many of the most beautiful

Fig. 105 Cheltenham, The Second Westholme, St George's Road – see page 152.

> of the modern ecclesiastical buildings in the neighbourhood. Mr. Middleton may be said to have died in harness. He left home a week before his death to visit some work he was carrying out for a gentleman in Newcastle Emlyn in South Wales, and being seized with paralysis, he quickly lapsed into unconsciousness and died at the home of the gentleman in whose interest the journey was undertaken.

The report continued:

> Mr. Middleton had been resident in Cheltenham for about 25 years, and during that period had been associated with much of the best work of a time of unusual architectural activity.

There followed a list of his most notable achievements in Cheltenham, a special reference to his work at Berkeley Castle and a passing reference to his work in Wales. *The Cheltenham Looker-On* also recorded his death in its edition of 14th February, the day after it had happened and made much of his architectural genius "to which Cheltenham is so largely indebted for its ecclesiastical edifices." Slightly more detail is included about the events surrounding his death:

> He was seized by paralysis, which deprived him at once of bodily and mental power and where he remained in a state of unconsciousness until his life became extinct early yesterday morning.

Middleton was supervising the building of the mansion at Newcastle Emlyn for Charles Fitzwilliams. As suggested in the earlier description of the work on this mansion, Cilgwyn, the relationship between client and architect was at times somewhat strained but little information about the events leading up to Middleton's stroke is available. The Coroner's records for that period have not survived and the only sequence of events is to be found in the diary of Captain Fitzwilliams held at the National Library of Wales, Aberystwyth, *Cilgwyn Estate Records (Group II)*

4th February 1885	Middleton did not come I went back to Tymawr. Carmarthen races.
Thursday 5th Feb.	Middleton came by evening bus.
Sat 7th February	Mr Middleton found ill in bed, paralytic stroke. Mrs Middleton and maid arrived.
Mon 9th February	Middleton very ill. Nurse White arrived from Onford Home.
Tues 10th February	Middleton very ill.
Wed 11th February	Sinking gradually.
Thurs 12th February	Near gone last night. Better today. H Middleton in town. Knocked up with journey. Must come

	on by first train.
	H Middleton arrives at 12.30 am.
Friday 13th Feb	Middleton died at 7 am.
Sat 14th February	Nurse White left.
Mon 16th February	Middletons left.
March 4th	Mr Prothero here.

His burial took place at the New Cemetery, Bouncers Lane, Cheltenham on February 18th.and the burials register for the Parish Church of St Mary records the name of the undertaker – Scannel; Middleton's age, sixty four; his religion, Established Church; and the fact that he was buried in a vault. The Reverend G. P. Griffiths, Vicar of Middleton's first Cheltenham Church, St Mark's, officiated at the funeral. Surprisingly, in view of Middleton's reputation in the town, the local press did not carry an account of the funeral service, nor a list of mourners.

Earlier reference has been made to the apparent severance of ties between John Middleton and Christ Church, where he had been an active member since his arrival in the town. Accepting the fact that his parish priest and friend of over twenty years, Canon Fenn had pre-deceased him, it is still puzzling that his funeral did not take place from Christ Church. *The Gloucestershire Echo* report of 19th February only adds to the mystery:

> The funeral of the late Mr Middleton took place on Wednesday morning at the Cemetery and in the evening a muffled peal consisting of 962 changes of Kent Treble Bob Majors was rung upon the Parish Church Bells by the Society of Ringers, Mr Belcher conducting.

Tributes were paid to his memory by many of those who had been colleagues in the many organisations to which he belonged in the town and beyond, the first and most poignant being that given at All Saints' Church by the Priest-in-Charge, the Reverend G. Gardner, on the Sunday following his death:

> Especially was grateful remembrance due to him from the congregation worshipping at All Saints, for the stately church which was the result of his taste and skill, and it might truly be said, of his deep religious feeling. No one could have the privilege of being personally acquainted with Mr Middleton without being strongly attracted by his gentle, childlike spirit, and at the same time his varied stores of information and his wide culture. The deepest sympathy must be felt for his widow and his son in the sorrow which has so unexpectedly overtaken them.

The Reverend Gardner also reminded his congregation that the beautiful House of God in which they were sitting was a fitting tribute to his memory and skill.

Of tributes paid by colleagues and friends, none was more moving than that paid by Major R. C. Barnard, who with Middleton was a founder member of the Cheltenham Library. He had employed Middleton to design his house, Bartlow, on Leckhampton Hill and he was also a very close personal friend. Middleton had served as Treasurer of the Library for twenty two years and at its Council Meeting shortly after his death had been announced, the following tribute was paid by Major Barnard:

> The points which particularly struck me were his perseverance and hopefulness and these were impressed by their influence upon the foundation and success of the Library. When the acknowledged want of such an Institution led me to make an effort to meet it, it was to Mr. Middleton that I first had recourse; and I shall never forget the readiness with which Mr. Middleton entered into the project and the perseverance and confidence with which he supported it. Often when the difficulties we met with caused my energy to flag, and made me despair of success, Mr. Middleton's hopefulness assured me, and we persevered in our undertaking. Very few of those who bore the early burden of the work now remain amongst us but none of these would feel that his work was disparaged when I say that it was due to Mr. Middleton more than to anyone else, that the Library was founded and that it has enjoyed so successful a career.

An expression of the Council's sincere sympathy with Mrs Middleton and her son was recorded and a copy sent to them. Other members of the Library Council remarked on the readiness with which Middleton had always placed his professional skill gratuitously at the service of the Council.

Not only in Cheltenham was his loss greatly mourned. Ewan Christian, a colleague, the architect of Cheltenham's St Matthew's Church, sometime Diocesan Architect and President of the Incorporated Church Building Society, when making his presidential speech to the RIBA in November 1885, made special mention of John Middleton:

> (He was) one of the kindest and most genial of men. He was an excellent architect, an artist and an antiquary some of whose works display, in combination with sound construction, a freshness of design which is always grateful to those who can appreciate good work.

His professional reputation is best summed up in quotations from the many publications which recorded his death:

> He possessed the ability to obtain the best results (viz St Mark's) with the minimum of expenditure, but also where costs were not limited, as at All Saints, Holy Apostles and St Stephen's, recently built and completed under his design and personal direction..... All through Wales his talent is illustrated by many striking works ... The Bishop of St David's relied much on his architectural judgement and taste.
>
> (*The Cheltenham Examiner* 18.02.1885)

> His name will become associated with the County of Gloucestershire for generations.
>
> (*The Cheltenham Looker-On* 14.02.1885)

> The Bristol and Gloucester Archaeological Society laments the death of Mr. John Middleton, Founder Member, Provisional Committee Member, Member of the Cheltenham Council Proper of the Society and local Secretary.
>
> (*BGAS Transactions* Vol 10 p3 1885/6)

> A year or two after settling in Cheltenham, he gratuitously made the design for All Saints Church, Cheltenham, which was so much admired that he was induced to commence

> practice again, and carried out the Ladies College, Cheltenham and a great many other works in the neighbourhood, having especially a large connection amongst the clergy in Wales.......He was devoted to his profession and several well known men were brought forward by him, amongst others Mr. Boulton the architectural sculptor.
>
> (*The Builder*, 21.02.1885)

> Of all the local church architects living in the Victorian period, none is as prolific as Middleton – nor more talented, with perhaps the exception of Benjamin Bucknall.
>
> (David Verey in Pevsner, *The Buildings of England:Gloucestershire, The Vale and the Forest of Dean)*

> He seems to have been a friendly, sociable man, winning friends from both sides of the ecclesiastical divide.
>
> (Christopher Bishop, *Presidential Address to the B G A S 1992)*

> Middleton's vision of creating (for Cheltenham) a medieval skyline of towers and spires was never fully to be realised, but his five churches .....stand today as his finest achievement, and most significant contribution to Cheltenham's Victorian architecture.
>
> (Hugh Greenhalf, *A Gloucestershire Gallery*)

John Middleton's burial place and memorial at Cheltenham Cemetery is not in any way ostentatious, being one in a row of many similar memorials north of the Chapel door. A simple plain cross bears the following legend on its plinth:

In memory of John Middleton, b 27 Aug 1820. d 13 Feb 1885.
Forever with the Lord
Jesus Mercy.

On the side of the plinth is also inscribed:

Also of
Maria Margaret, his wife
Who died Dec 23rd 1898
Aged 81 years.

Little has been said about Maria Margaret apart from casual references to her presence at official openings or fund raising events. It will be remembered that John and Maria had only just bought and moved into Gresham House, St George's Road when he died so suddenly in Wales. Already the house had been renamed 'Westholme', announced as such in *The Cheltenham Looker-On* of 3rd January 1885. The new owners of Middleton's former home in Overton Road continued to call that Westholme too at least until April 1885. The name was later changed to Abbeyholme and the circumstances surrounding this change have already been explained. We have no information as to who was present at Middleton's funeral, but afterwards Mrs Middleton travelled to Yorkshire to spend some time with her family, returning to Cheltenham on July 11th 1885. She was soon joined by her son John Henry who was at this time, living and working in Cambridge. The Yorkshire visit must have been an emotional one for Mrs Middleton as just eight months previously, in June 1884, she had accompanied her husband on a holiday visit to family and friends in that area. In widowhood Mrs Middleton continued to visit friends and relatives and the year after her husband's death she is recorded in the Cheltenham arrivals list as having just 'returned from St Leonard's on Sea and Rugby.'

Maria Middleton continued to live at Westholme until 1893 and the arrivals/departures lists for Cheltenham record her visits to and returns from London until that time. By 1894 she had moved to the capital to live with her son, daughter-in-law and granddaughter. John Henry had only just been appointed Art Director of the South Kensington Museum. Their reunion was not to last for long. John Henry died in 1896 after which Maria Middleton continued to live in the city near her daughter-in-law and granddaughter for a further two years. On 23rd December 1898 Maria Margaret Middleton died aged eighty-one years. Her cremated remains were brought back to Cheltenham and were interred on 29th December in the grave in which her husband was buried.

Probate records give her address at the time of death as 22, Kensington Court Mansions, Middlesex, and probate was granted on 18th January 1899 to Thomas Henry Morris J P, and Richard Charles Pritchett, accountant, her nephew. Maria and her son John Henry had been the sole beneficiaries under the will of John Middleton senior, a will which had been drawn up in 1882. At that time his share holdings consisted of one seventeenth of the North Bitchburn Colliery in Durham, and the house in Cheltenham together with its contents. No mention is made in the will of the architectural practice. Maria was left whatever of the household contents she decided to keep and personal effects. The shares income was to be equally divided between her and John Henry and upon the death of either, their share would pass to their respective heirs. There was one proviso, namely that should Maria's income not maintain £600 per annum, it was to be made up from her son's shares income. Neither party could sell shares while the other was still alive without mutual agreement. Probate was granted in September 1885 to the value of £16,643.8.5, a comfortable amount equivalent to well over one and a half million pounds in today's purchasing value. John Henry, although the potential successor to the architectural practice, never felt entirely at home in the profession and his interest in Art and Archaeology eventually persuaded him to relinquish his share in the practice and to pursue those interests which ultimately made him more famous nationally than his father had been. This happened about 1889.

A letter to the Incorporated Church Building Society from Ewan Christian with reference to John Henry Middleton's work on the church at Capel Bach, in 1886, explained that "Middleton is very able, but has dedicated himself to archaeology." It would seem appropriate to conclude this study of the life of John Middleton with a short account of the life of his only child, his son John Henry and of his sad and untimely death.

Sources consulted:

National Library of Wales, Cilgwyn (II) 72.

GA, P78/1 CW3/6/7

The Cheltenham Examiner 11th March 1885. The Library was the Permanent Library for which subscriptions had to be paid.

CHAPTER XXVIII

John Henry Middleton

Fig. 106 John Henry Middleton

John Henry Middleton was the only child of John Middleton and Maria, nee Pritchett. The *Gloucester Journal* of 20th June 1896 reported in his obituary that prior to his arrival in Cheltenham he had received his early education in Italy and this is repeated in his obituary in *The Times*. It would appear that he spent some time touring that country with his parents and studied at the school attached to the Benedictine Abbey of La Cava near Naples. This early experience of the country obviously inspired in him an affection which was to last to the end of his life. It is no surprise that on his arrival in Cheltenham in 1859 or perhaps as late as 1861, he could speak fluent Italian as well as his native tongue. His years at Cheltenham College as a day boy, August 1861 until December 1864, and his Oxford days, were not outstanding and he left Exeter College without a Degree after just over a year there. This was as the result of depression caused by the sudden death of a very close fellow student. John Henry returned to the family home in Cheltenham and spent the following five or six years deep in study, which must have caused his parents some concern as he kept very much to himself and made very few friends. He was very much a loner who suffered from long bouts of depression and isolation. He had never been very healthy and was lean and fragile in appearance right up to the end of his life. The reading and study he did in these Cheltenham years between roughly 1866 – 1871, laid the foundation for his extensive knowledge of Art and Archaeology, for which he was in later years so highly respected. However there must have been some interest shown in his father's practice and no doubt he accompanied him and his partner Mr Goodman on site visits to restoration work or new projects. But Art and Archaeology fascinated him and memories of the things he had seen in Italy must have stirred up in him the urge to explore much further afield. The *Dictionary of National Biography* tells how he spent some years visiting America, Mexico, Greece, Asia Minor, Egypt and North Africa and he must have been a determined and courageous traveller for "he gained entry into the Great Mosque at Fez in Morocco, disguised as a pilgrim and gaining an audience with the Sultan, both feats previously unaccomplished by any one other than a Muslim."

In 1873 he set off for Iceland and on the boat he met William Morris and James Faulkner, one of Morris' partners. Morris' subsequent letters make many references to John Henry and a strong friendship had obviously developed between them which lasted to the end of their lives, both dying in 1896. Middleton spent weekends at Morris' home, Kelmscott in Oxfordshire, one of the many house-guests who were to become famous for their contribution to the Arts and Crafts Movement. He also accompanied Morris on walking or train expeditions to many of the Cotswold villages, such as Burford, sometimes staying overnight at places like Minster Lovell. What their conversation was about does not need much imagination but considering the vast amount of church restoration and rebuilding with which the Middleton firm was involved, and also knowing of Morris' strong opinions about such restoration, the atmosphere must have been at times quite heavy. However although frequent, the visits were often very short. Morris' letters illustrate the point - "John Middleton came on Sunday but only stayed his usual short time afterwards," and "Middleton called today but as usual went away very early". Incidentally, Morris often used the familiar name of Jack when talking and writing about John Henry to close friends

Perhaps to test his vocation, perhaps out of loyalty to his father, John Henry Middleton returned to London after his wanderings abroad and spent some time studying in the offices of George Gilbert Scott for which his father paid a tuition fee of £1,000. There he appears to have spent his time mainly on church work. From 1875 his London address was 122 Mount Street, Grosvenor Square, until he set up a branch office for his father's firm in 1877 at 4 Storey's Gate, almost half way between Horse Guards Parade and Westminster Abbey. This office continued until 1886. He must have made a favourable impression on Scott for when in 1875 he was elected RIBA Scott was one of his proposers together with F. P. Cockerell and his father's former partner and brother in law, J. P. Pritchett, his own uncle. Living in the heart of London, he was able to develop friendships with Rossetti and Burne-Jones for example, and his extensive knowledge made him a much respected source for advice about ancient buildings. In his later years he became secretary to the Society for the Protection of Ancient Buildings, a William Morris initiative and served on the committee in 1890 with many well known contemporaries such as S. C. Cockerell, William de Morgan, W. Holman Hunt, and E. Burne-Jones. He accompanied Morris on many site visits writing and signing reports on works to be done on ancient churches. According to *Kelvin*, some of these reports were quite scathing in their comments and recommendations and it was a well known fact that no architect was safe from criticism if Morris and Middleton thought it was deserved.

However his real passion in life was still Art and Archaeology. He followed a course at the Royal Academy, wrote articles for learned journals, gave lectures and conducted field excursions to ancient buildings. Some of these activities involved returning to Gloucestershire and he was a regular contributor to the meetings and the Transactions of the Bristol and Gloucestershire Archaeological Society. At the 1879 Annual Meeting of the County Archaeological Society held at the Plough Hotel in Cheltenham, a three-day event, he, as secretary, organised the programme and delivered a paper on, and led a site visit to Cheltenham's medieval parish church. Earlier, in 1872 it will be remembered, he was greatly involved with his father in the discovery and subsequent restoration and preservation of the frescoes at Kempley Church, Gloucestershire. He wrote a paper on the frescoes just before his journey to Iceland with Morris. He was elected Fellow of the Society of Antiquaries in 1879 and Vice President in 1894. Amidst all these activities he continued to travel abroad, especially in Italy, which he once visited with Morris to study the work being done on the restoration of St Mark's, Venice. He made many drawings while on these travels, carried out some excavation work and eventually published his findings. Was his father delighted at his son's rewarding interest and developing reputation or did he regret the passing of his hopes that his son might eventually take over and continue the practice? This we will never know as no Middleton diary has come to light.

However John Henry certainly maintained an interest in his father's practice and he continued to be involved with the life of Cheltenham and the county. In the 1870s he and his father became members of the Cheltenham Freemasons Foundation Lodge No 82. He involved himself with several county antiquarian societies. He also enjoyed artistic design and undertook several commissions. It has already been seen that he designed the altar frontal, lectern and probably the pulpit for Sowerby Church in Yorkshire; an altar frontal for All Saints Church in Cheltenham; and in 1880 he designed an elaborate oak mantelpiece which was carved by Martyn and Emms of Cheltenham, and exhibited at the Bath and West of England Local Art, Sculpture and Carving Exhibition. Just prior to this commission he had designed a fine oak chair for the Bishop of St David's, again carved by Martyn and Emms, and the oak desk presented to the Bishop when, as Archdeacon of York, his appointment to the See of St David was announced, may well have been to his design, rather than to that of his father.

L. W. Barnard recalled his first day working under John Henry when he took over the practice following the death of his father in 1885.

"I was met by him and a staff which consisted of 6 or 8 assistants. John Henry gave me at once a job to copy a church plan and after a short time came to see what I had done. He thoroughly scared me by exclaiming that I had done nothing and when he saw my writing and printing I thought he was never going to stop. When he went out of the room, his assistants assured me that that was nothing new as he always expected everyone to work as fast as he did. It startled me for the first day at work but I must say however that he was kindness itself. When he took his pupils out one at a time to see work, he could not take too much trouble to answer any questions and to teach as much as possible." This latter compliment was confirmed in later years by John Henry's friends and colleagues in the William Morris circle.

John Henry soon admitted however, that provincial architectural practice was not for him, although after his father's death in 1885, he continued in the business for a while with his father's recently acquired partners, H. Prothero and G. Phillott. The partnership maintained branches in Cheltenham, Newport (Monmouthshire) from where Prothero came, and Westminster. The Newport address of Middleton, Prothero and Phillott was Albion Chambers, Commercial Street until at least 1890.

Shortly after his father's death, John Henry Middleton, at the age of 40, was elected Slade Professor of Fine Art at Cambridge, a position to which he was twice re-elected between 1886 and 1895. He was given the Honorary Degree MA (Cantab) in 1886 and MA (Oxon) in 1887. In 1888 he was elected Fellow of Kings College Cambridge, an honour also once held by his maternal great-grandfather. The practice address then changed to Cambridge, Cheltenham and Newport, Mon. In 1889 he was appointed Director of the Fitzwilliam Museum, a post he held in addition to his other positions. He was now able to devote more time to writing and publishing the wealth of knowledge he had gained in his short life. Among these publications were numerous contributions to the new edition of the Encyclopaedia Britannica, some published jointly with William Morris, and 'Ancient Rome'. *The Athenaeum* reported that there was hardly any subject connected with the history of art and archaeology upon which John Henry was not well informed and upon many, he proved that he was an authority. *Anthony Burton* found that this is supported in the Testimonials in favour of John Henry Middleton as candidate for the Slade Professorship at Cambridge in 1886, to succeed Sidney Colvin. His own covering letter refers to his many publications, including books, articles and encyclopaedia entries for which many of the illustrations were from his own drawings and his appraisal of his career up to 1886 mentions his study of art as a student in Paris and Rome. He also revealed an impressive list of interests and accomplishments, supporting the belief that he was indeed a devotee of the ancient and the aesthetic rather than the contemporary and functional.

Burton lists John Henry's supporters for the professorship, amongst whom were Sidney Colvin of the British Museum; the Dean of Westminster; several university Fellows or Tutors; the Director of the National Gallery, Sir Frederick Burton; William Morris and Edward Burne-Jones.

Morris' confirmation of his support was given in a letter to John Henry, quoted in *Kelvin*, and written in February 1886:

Dear M, hear you are a candidate for the vacant Slade Professorship. I consider you thoroughly qualified for the post which seems to me requires a man of your accurate and detailed knowledge of Art and Archaeology. I am sure you will bring your extraordinary painstaking industry to bear on the work you would do if elected.

Sidney Colvin's comments in his favour emphasised his "great retentiveness of eye and mind and conclusions based on soundness of knowledge rather than ingenuity of speculation" and A. J. Butler, Fellow and Tutor, Brasenose College, Oxford wrote that,

> "...in other departments of medieval art, whether concerned with bronzes or ivories, coins or gems, pottery or porcelain, gold or silver work, with mosaics, enamels or textiles, his mind is as well furnished as if each had been his single study. In Oriental Art he ranks as one of the few English experts. In ecclesiology his learning and research are justly famous." (*The Athenaeum*)

Middleton's nomination was approved as we know, and perhaps his colleagues and friends hoped that this new challenge might in some way take his mind off the death of his father just a year previously and provide some escape from his mental and physical health concerns. He obviously felt the loss of his father very deeply and Morris who had seen him in Oxford wrote to his daughter of his worries about him. Writing from Hammersmith in March 1885, just over a month after Middleton senior's death, Morris told her that he had seen John Henry in Oxford for only a few minutes where he was on some matter to do with his father's death. He described how ill he looked especially since having grown a woeful looking beard.

A contemporary letter from Jane Morris to her close friend Wilfrid Scawen Blunt, written in May 1889, gives one an insight into his personality: "People either like him extremely or not at all, he is a great favourite with all of us, but we see little of him he is such a busy worker. I was almost sorry when he was re-elected Slade Professor last year. Still he is paid for that and he is not for much of his work. I never can think of him belonging to this century, or Western civilisation at all, he is like a bit of old world thought and feeling re-embodied and wafted from the East."

In addition to being twice re-elected to the Professorship and being Director of the Fitzwilliam Museum, he also became at the same time, a lecturer at London's Royal Academy, yet he still found time for travel. Jane Morris writing to W. S. Blunt in February 1892 informed him that Middleton would be leaving in a fortnight's time to spend three months in Greece. Later that year, he was on a visit to Rome, where he took great delight in conducting friends and tourists around the ancient historical ruins. Jane, again writing to Blunt informed him that she had received a letter from JHM telling her that he had proposed to Bella Stillman, daughter of the Times correspondent in Italy, and had been accepted. They married in Rome in December 1892, just before he took up his appointment as Director of Art at the South Kensington Museum. Bella was twenty years his junior, but their married life was a happy and supportive one and they were blessed with one child, a daughter Mary Margaret – 'Peggy'. Her birth, "to Dr Middleton's wife," in March 1894, was announced in *The Cheltenham Examiner,* suggesting that the Middletons still maintained contact with friends and colleagues in the town. A further letter in March the following year, again to Blunt, told him that Middleton and his bride had visited Jane's family in London, and that they were seeking a suitable piece of land on which to build a nest for themselves.

Walter James Stillman, John Henry's father-in-law, was born in New York State in 1828. He was keenly interested in art and related studies and as a young man he edited an Art Journal in New York, called *Crayon*, in response to Ruskin's popularity in the USA. He had heard about the exciting things happening in England in the Art world and moved to England to take up painting as a career. Stillman met and eventually married the daughter of a Cambridge doctor. They returned to America and Stillman accepted the post of US Consul in Rome. He was later appointed US Consul in Crete, but in 1868 they moved to Athens where his wife committed suicide in grief over the atrocities which had been perpetrated against the Christians in Crete. Stillman was left a widower with three children - two daughters, Lisa and Bella, and a son to whom he was devoted. Because of his son's serious hip disease, Stillman returned to England and sought out his former art contacts, for a while sharing a house with D. G. Rossetti. It was through these contacts that he met, and married in 1871, Miss Marie Spartali, the daughter of the Greek Consul in London.

Marie was fifteen years his junior and closely involved professionally and personally with the pre-Raphaelite Circle. Marie had been born in England into a very wealthy and socially important family, a family which became sponsors of the pre-Raphaelite movement. According to Jan Marsh and Pamela Nunn, the marriage was strongly opposed by her family because of the difference in their ages, and because he was a widower with three children. Their first child was born the following year. In 1875, Stillman went as volunteer war correspondent for the Times to cover the anti-Turkish uprising in the Balkans. From there he moved to Italy continuing as correspondent for the newspaper, leaving Marie in England with their own daughter Euphrosyne, and her step-daughters. Three years later she joined Stillman in Florence where they settled and where their son Michael was born. William Morris and his wife visited them there in 1880. The Stillmans seemed to spend their time moving between Italy and Greece but in 1886 Stillman and his family made Rome their base and lived there for the next ten years. The family at this time comprised Walter, Marie, their two children Euphrosyne (Effie) and Michael, and the two girls by his first marriage, Lisa and Bella whom Marie treated as if they were her own. The girls too often visited Morris at Kelmscott when they were in England and it is probably safe to assume that it was through his contacts with Morris that John Henry Middleton first met Marie Spartali and Lisa and Bella Stillman and it is even more probable that during his many visits to Italy, Rome in particular, he met Walter Stillman and the larger family.

Director of Art at the South Kensington Museum was a new post, created upon the separation of the former Science and Art Department. Middleton was 'head hunted' to fill the position and accepted the challenge with obvious enthusiasm. His role was to modernise the Department, rearrange the displays and add to its treasures, many new exhibits being bought on his recommendation. This of course added to his national and international reputation and perhaps the added pressure contributed to his early death.

It was at this time that his mother, Maria, moved from Cheltenham to London and his health may have been one of the reasons for her move. Jane Morris, William's wife, writing to W. S. Blunt in July 1894 remarked that she had seen John Henry just a day or so previously and how hopelessly ill he looked to her way of thinking. He spent a lot of time out of doors, walking or resting, and seemed totally lifeless .His wife Bella read to him for several hours each day and now and again he dictated letters to her. In Jane's opinion he had lost interest in everything apart from wife and baby and if it were not for them he would not seek medical help. He took sick leave for a year spending most of it in Italy, and while there his health deteriorated quite dramatically. Jane Morris again, writing about him in February 1895, said that he was little better than when he left England. He eventually returned to London, but the strain of his work, brought on further attacks of the depression which he had experienced in his youth and for the relief of which he had resorted to the use of morphia.

On Monday 15th June 1896, *The Times* carried the report of the enquiry into the sad circumstances surrounding the death of Professor John Henry Middleton, DCL, aged

49, Director of Art at the South Kensington Museum. He had died at 2, Museum Residences, Exhibition Road, South Kensington, on 10th June. The cause of death was an overdose of morphia. Mr J Winterbotham, solicitor of Cheltenham, watched the case on behalf of Middleton's family and there were several friends of the deceased in the Court. It was stated that he had been at his post at the museum for only three years and he was an MA and DCL of Oxford University. His body had been identified by Mr Richmond Thackeray Ritchie of the India Office. He had last seen the deceased in February but was well informed of the deceased's illness as his wife was an intimate friend of the family. Ritchie was one of the executors of Middleton's will and confirmed that his life was insured for £2000.

Middleton's widow Bella was asked to take the stand and she described the head pains which he had had for the past three years and which the doctor put down to depression. John Henry had disagreed with this diagnosis and believed that there was something wrong with his brain. Recently he had been victim to insomnia and loss of appetite. He had seen a specialist who confirmed that he was not suffering delusions and that there was definitely no organic disorder. Mrs Middleton explained that as an undergraduate he had had brain fever and his life was despaired of for want of sleep. He had therefore been prescribed morphia three times a day but had become so anxious that he purchased large quantities of it so that he would never be in a position of not having any at hand. His doctors had told him to come off it or else he stood no chance of getting better but he admitted that this was not possible.

His widow explained that on the previous Tuesday he had had two doses, one at eleven am and one at three pm. He usually took a third dose before bed time. She read to him during the evening and he seemed cheerful when he retired to bed at the usual time of 9 pm. There had been no disturbance during the night and when she went out next day, she did not wake him. On her return at 6 pm she found two doctors in attendance, and John Henry lying unconscious. He died the same night. The inquest report confirmed that he had been on morphia for 22 years, since the age of 27, and was addicted to it. He had possibly, unintentionally taken an overdose as he could not sleep. The body was extremely emaciated but the brain was healthy and there was nothing abnormal to report. Death was undoubtedly due to a coma from morphia poisoning and a verdict of 'Death from Misadventure' was recorded.

Kelvin quotes the diary of W. S. Blunt of June 17th 1896 which refers to Middleton's death and his opinion was that it had the appearance of suicide. He deplored his death as a great loss, although as far as his friends were concerned, he had been dead to the world for something like two years. However *The Times* report of the inquest, referred to above, quoted the doctor who had been attending John Henry for two and a half years – " I do not think his death was in any way intentional." The Harley Street doctor who had carried out the autopsy confirmed that he had found evidence of Bright's kidney disease. Immediately after the inquest the body of John Henry Middleton was taken by rail to Woking and cremated by the deceased's own wish. Only a few friends and relatives were present. Of his relatives, there may have been some from his mother's side of the family but from available evidence, it would appear that his father had none living at the time. Whether his in-laws, the Stillmans returned from

Italy we do not know, but John Henry's ashes were buried on 13th June in Plot 2S at Brookwood Cemetery, Woking. In adjacent plots are buried his father-in-law who died in 1901, his mother-in-law Marie Spartali Stillman who died in 1927 and in John Henry's plot, his sister-in-law, Lisa Stillman who died in 1946.

Many were the published appreciations of John Henry's life among which was that of the Society of Antiquaries of London, to which he had been elected Fellow in 1879 and Vice President in 1894 and *The American Architect* also devoted much space to his obituary.

Morris received the news of John Henry's death on the train on his way to Folkestone. He spent June 1896 in Folkestone, and his health was affected by the news of his friend's death. He and Middleton had much in common and Morris admired Middleton's obvious and sincere friendliness to those whom he considered close to him. Jane Morris wrote to W. S. Blunt that news of John Henry's death "threw (her) over for the day. I knew of poor Mr Middleton's habit, (opium). I discovered it soon after we first knew him. He nearly killed himself then but his mother came and carried him off and had him nursed. I wonder that Bella ever left the bottle within his reach."

John Henry Middleton had written his will just six months before his death, on December 18th 1895. His appointed executors were his wife Bella and his friends Thomas Henry Morris JP of The Lodge, Halifax and Richmond Ritchie Esq., of The India Office, London. In the event of Bella surviving him, he left everything to her. Naturally he also appointed her sole guardian of their only child Mary Margaret. Should Bella die at the same time as he did, then three trustees, Thomas Henry Morris, Richmond Ritchie and his friend Somers Clarke of 3, Whitehall Court, London, " were to administer the estate on behalf of Mary Margaret until she reach the age of 25, or upon her prior marriage". His wife's sisters, Lisa and Effie Stillman were appointed joint guardians within the above terms relating to age and marriage. Maintenance was to be paid by the trustees out of the income of the Trust, for the daughter and for the guardians' expenses. Should Lisa or Effie die before Mary Margaret reached the rightful age of inheritance, then the trustees were appointed to fulfil the guardians' role in their place. Should Mary Margaret die before the realisation of the bequest, the estate was to be shared between Marie Spartali Stillman, his mother-in-law, and Lisa and Effie Stillman, his sisters-in-law.

The witnesses to the will were Caspar Purdon Clarke, Assistant Director of the South Kensington Museum and Arthur Banks Skinner, Keeper of the Museum. Probate was granted on 12th August 1896, the value net being £18,217.0.6. The final value, resworn in October of that year amounted to £23,052.4.5. No mention was made in the will of John Henry's mother who was living near him in South Kensington and who did not die until two years after him in 1898. Of the executors, Richmond Ritchie was the same person who had given evidence at the inquest and had identified the body. Thomas Henry Morris was the son of William and Barbara Morris, William being the founder of the firm of worsted spinners, William Morris and Sons, of Sowerby Bridge. They were married in York in 1846 and were friends of John Middleton senior. Their son Thomas was a contemporary of young John Henry and in 1861 it is recorded that Thomas aged 13, was staying with the Middletons in Cheltenham on census night.

John Middleton senior was spared the unpleasant publicity surrounding his son's death but sadly did not live to witness his son's marriage nor to see his grand-daughter, Mary Margaret (Peggy). Of John Henry's career and involvement with the firm little actual evidence exists. Plans bearing the legend "Middleton and Son" begin with the restoration of Charlton Kings Parish Church in 1876. Those signed 'Henry Middleton' include library work for a large mansion, The Elms, Darlington, 1878; Kempley Church Record of Mural Paintings by H. Middleton, not dated; the altar frontals for Sowerby and All Saints, Cheltenham, already mentioned and Broadway Church alterations 1889. It was at about this time that he retired from active involvement with the firm, although it continued as Middleton, Prothero and Phillott until the year of his death.

The Building News of 1890 in celebrating his Directorship of the Fitzwilliam Museum at Cambridge, does however credit him with a considerable contribution to the second phase of the designs for the Cheltenham Ladies' College, and to the work at Ss Phillip and James Church, Cheltenham, the Picture Gallery at Hampton Court House, and both Coleshill Court and Beckford Hall. In partnership with Prothero and Phillott he was responsible for the additions to St David's College mentioned earlier; the completion of Trinity Church Aberystwyth; the Red House, Oxford and the major alterations to the east end of Christ Church, Cheltenham. I quote Christopher Bishop:

> "The only building for which we can be certain that he was responsible, in Cheltenham, was the adaptation of the Regency Gothic Christ Church, into an Early Christian Roman Basilica. I like to visualise him working in his set of rooms in the Fellows' Building at King's, sending his drawings back to Cheltenham for working up by his partners' assistant. There are cryptic notes such as "Romanesque Corinthian Capitals; see Bramente's Cancellaria in small note book," and " Memo, no cross over altar" a reminder of the problem of imposing a high Roman style of architecture on a Cheltenham Evangelical congregation".

How appropriate that the son should leave his mark on Cheltenham in the very church in which his father first worshipped on his arrival in Cheltenham and which he served as Churchwarden for twenty-five years.

Both *The Athenaeum* and *The Academy* provide the ultimate testimonials to one of Cheltenham's most respected adopted sons:

> At Cambridge he did far more than fulfil the bare requirements of his professorship and there and elsewhere he was always ready with help and advice for those who sought them of him, and his death will be felt as the loss of a friend by many, in many parts of the world. There is little doubt that Middleton toiled beyond his strength for the greater part of his life, and that when he went to South Kensington, he was not equal to the hard work which had to be done there. (*The Athenaeum*)

> The characteristic of all his books is the intimate acquaintance shown with technical processes. For in truth, Middleton was not so much a scholar in the German sense, as a trained observer with a keen, sympathetic eye, and an unusual power of lucid exposition...It remains to say that Middleton possessed in the happier periods of his life, a genius

> for friendship. He would devote himself to the service of others – even when they had little claim on him - with an affection that was almost feminine. At the same time he could burn with righteous anger against whatever was base in conduct or in art. His character indeed was half Italian, strengthened by the religion of Positivism, which, at one period at least, exercised a powerful influence upon him. (*The Academy*)

John Henry's widow, Bella continued to live in London and died a widow in Chelsea in August 1948 at the age of eighty. Mary Margaret, (Peggy), Bella and John Henry's only child married Louis Reynolds but they had no children. She died in the 1960s.

Sources consulted:

Correspondence with Sarah Medlam, V&A Museum, London.
Information provided through Sarah Medlam, by Anthony Burton, V&A Museum, London.
Burton, Anthony, *Vision and Accident, the Story of the Victoria and Albert Museum*.
Entry for John Henry Middleton in *Dictionary of National Biography*.
The Athenaeum, 20th June 1896
The Academy, 20th June 1896.
The Architect and Contract Reporter, 19th June 1896.
The Times, obituary of Walter Stillman, 9th September 1901.
The Times, obituary of Marie Stillman 8th March 1927.
Brookwood Cemetery Records, Woking.
London Probate Record Office 6th March 1927.
The American Architect Vol. 53 1896, p10.
West Yorkshire Archive Service, Calderdale, re Thomas Henry Morris.
Royal Institute of British Architects *Biographical File, John Henry Middleton.*
Royal Institute of British Architects, *Transactions*, 1886, p11.
Cheltenham Masonic Records.
The Cheltenham Examiner 23rd June 1880.
Conversations and correspondence with the late Christopher Bishop, RIBA.
Faulkner, Peter, (ed) *Jane Morris to Wilfrid Scawen Blunt.* All quotations from these letters are taken from Faulkner's book, with kind permission.
Marsh, J and Nunn, P. G, *Women Artists and the pre-Raphaelite Movement.*
Barnard, L. W. *Ninety Years Past.*
Cox, Anna Somers, *The Victoria and Albert Museum: The Making of The Collection.*
Kelvin, Norman, *(ed) The Collected Letters of William Morris.*
Lindsay, Jack, *Biography of William Morris.*
Bristol and Gloucestershire Archaeological Society *Transactions.*
Building News. February 1890.
Elliott, David B, *A Pre-Raphaelite Marriage, The Lives and Works of Marie Spartali Stillman & Walter James Stillman.* 2006.

BIBLIOGRAPHY

The Early Years: THE NORTH of ENGLAND

Alston-Watson, G. *The Centenary History of Ayton School 1941.* Hindley Bros.

Anon. *Jubilee Memorial of the Railway System – The History of the Stockton and Darlington Railway 1875.*

Broadbent, G. *Studies in Architectural History, Vol. II.* York Institute of Architectural Study. 1956.

Chapman, Vera. *Rural Darlington.* Durham County Council. 1975.
Darlington, Birthplace of the Railways. Discovery Publishing UK.

Cleveland & Teesside Local History Society. *Saints Alive.* 1994.

Cockcroft, Janet. *Redcar and Coatham.* 1976.

Colvin, H. *A Biographical Dictionary of English Architects.* 1978.

Dixon, George. *Jubilee History of Ayton School.* Privately published. 1891.

Dixon, Roger and Muthesius, Stefan. *Victorian Architecture.* Thames and Hudson 1978.

Elliott, John. *Ecclesiology Today,* No 12. January 1997.

Fawcett, Bill. *A History of NE Railway Architecture. Vol. I The Pioneers.* NER Association 2001.

Flynn, G. *Darlington in Old Picture Postcards.* European Library. Vol. I 1990; Vol. II 1994.
The Book of Darlington. Baracuda Books 1987.

Harper, Roger. *Index to British and Irish Architectural Competitions in The Builder.* Mansell Publications 1983.

Langstaffe, W. H. D., FSA. *The History and Antiquities of Darlington.* n.d.

Moore, Tommy. *Consett, A Town in the Making.* County Durham Books 1992.

Moorsom, Norman. *Journey Through the History of Middlesbrough.* Privately Published 1993.

O'Sullivan, Dan. *Great Ayton, A History of the Village.* Privately Published 1983.

Orde, Anne. *Religion, Business and Society in NE England.* Shaun Tyas. 2000.

Pease, Sir Alfred, (Editor.) *The Diary of Edward Pease.* Headley Bros. 1907.

Pevsner, Sir Nikolaus. *The Buildings of England. Yorkshire and the North Riding. Durham.*

Philo, Phil. *Redcar. A Pictorial History.* Phillimore. 1993.
Kirkleatham. Langbaurgh Borough Council. n.d.

Plummer, G. *The History of St John The Evangelist, 1847 – 1997.* Privately published.

Royle, Edward. (Editor). *A History of the Nonconformist Churches of York. Borthwick Texts and Calendars, No18 (1993).*

Sharp, Sir Cuthbert, FSA. *The History of Hartlepool.* 1851.

Simmons, E. J. *The Stockton and Darlington Railway and What Followed.* Methuen 1975.

Spence, M, and Everatt, M. *A Short History of York.* A Brown & Son. 1948.
Taylor, Jeremy. *The Architectural Medal.* British Museum 1977.
University of York, Borthwick Institute of Historical Research.1993. *Borthwick Texts and Calendars No 18.*
Walbran, J. *Redcar. A Visitors' Guide.*1848.
Workers' Educational Association. *Aspects of Darlington, 1850 – 1851.* Darlington 1999.
Woodhouse, Robert. *Darlington, A Pictorial History.* Phillimore. 1998.

DIRECTORIES

Baines, *Yorkshire Directory* 1823.
Blue Guide *Architecture in Britain.*
Churches Conservation Trust *Holy Trinity Church, Goodramgate, York.* n.d.
County of Durham Directory 1851, 1865, 1894.
Directory of the N.E Riding. 1872.
Hull and York Directory 1851.
Kelly's Directories – relevant years and areas acknowledged in text.
Pearson and White, *Directory 1830.*
RIBA. *Directory of British Architects, 1834-1900.*
Slater's Directory 1848.
St Nicholas Church, Durham. *Church Guide.*
Whellan, F. *Historical and Topographical Directory of Durham* 1856.
White's Directory 1847.

JOURNALS, PERIODICALS, ARTICLES and PAMPHLETS

Bricks and Mortar – A Celebration of Architecture in Hartlepool. Museum Services 1984.
Builder,The. Various editions as acknowledged in the text.
City of York Royal Commission on Historic Monuments.
Civil Engineer and Architects' Journal 1850.
Ecclesiologist. Vol. XII.
Journal of the Wesley Historical Society, N.E Branch 1990. *The Diary of F.R.N. Haswell for 1853,* ed Geoffrey Milburn.
Middlesbrough Borough Council: *Middlesbrough Heritage – Echoes of the Past.* n.d.
Stockton on Tees Library. *Railway Stations of Clevedon, No 1, Clevedon Rail Corridor Improvement Scheme.*

LOCAL and COUNTY NEWSPAPERS

Individual dates of reference are to be found in the notes after each chapter.

Darlington & Stockton Times 1851; *Durham Advertiser* 1847; *Newcastle Courant* 1847; *Northeast Journal* 1957; *Northern Dispatch* 1962; *Northern Echo* 1994, 1996; *Ripon & Richmond Chronicle* 1911; *York Advertiser* 1853; *Yorkshire Gazette*, 1855.

ARCHIVE MATERIAL

University of York, Borthwick Institute of Historical Research, York. Marriage, Baptism and Burial Registers for Holy Trinity Church, Goodramgate, York.

Census Return for the City of York 1841.

Copy of Wills held at the University of York, Borthwick Institute of Historical Research, York.

Court of Probate, York District.

Parliamentary Voters' Lists for the City of York 1841.

The following Local History Centres and Archive Departments have been consulted in person or by post and have been most helpful in supplying information, photocopying documents and suggesting further lines of enquiry. I am most grateful for the cheerful and willing assistance I have received at all times.

Council for the Care of Churches, Janet Seeley, Librarian.

Darlington – Ken Hoole Study Centre.

Darlington Library Local Studies Centre.

Durham County Archive Collection at County Hall for material on Piercebridge ; Hurworth; North Bitchburn Colliery; West Auckland Brewery; St John's Darlington.

Durham University Library, Diocesan Archives and Special Collections for Church Commissioners Parsonage House Plans, Darlington St John; Hartlepool; Coniscliffe, 1851, Greatham.

Teesside Archives, Middlesbrough.

Middlesbrough Reference Library.

Newcastle-Upon-Tyne Library, Local Studies Department.

North Yorkshire County Record Office, for Manfield Archives, and Ayton School.

Stockton-on-Tees Reference Library, Local Studies Department.

Torquay Reference Library.

York City Reference Library.

York City Archives.

York Minster Archives, Mrs C Harbisher, Inventory Secretary.

ACKNOWLEDGEMENTS

I have received much help and encouragement from so many people who have freely shared with me the fruits of their own research, providing photographs, newspaper cuttings, memories and suggestions for further lines of enquiry; making personal contacts on my behalf and in some cases offering me the hospitality of their own homes.

Mrs Vera Chapman, of Darlington; Miss Margaret Cumbor of Ayton, for invaluable help and hospitality; Bill Fawcett without whose help the section on Middleton's Railway work would have been very superficial indeed; Mr Mrs Harding of Cheltenham for information and photographs of Torquay and Torquay Local History Society for information and photograph of a drinking fountain designed by Middleton; Mr Geoffrey Milburn of Sunderland; Mr J. V. Mitchell, Hon. Archivist of St Peter's School, Clifton, York; Mr G. Potts, of High Shincliffe, Durham; Mr G. Gerard Wakeman, Assistant Archivist of Bootham (Quaker) School, York. Mr J. Wheeler of Middleton St George, Darlington; the Incumbents of the churches featured in this research for their willingness to provide time and resource material; the owners of Coniscliffe 'Vicarage' and of Neasham Hill for their hospitality.

The CHELTENHAM YEARS: WORK in GLOUCESTERSHIRE

Ambler, Lilian. *All Saints Church, Cheltenham*. c1959.
Armstrong, B.E. *St Mary Magdalene's Church*, Twyning. 1979.
Atherton, Eva. *Coberley, A History of the Church and Village*. 1994.
Andrew, Eve & Brewin, Eric. *Leckhampton Through the Ages*. 1984.
Barnard, L.W. *St Peter's Church, Leckhampton*. c1930.
Bick, David. *Old Newent and District*. 1992.
Bird, W.H. *Old Gloucestershire Churches*. n.d.
Blake, Steven. *Cheltenham, A Pictorial History*. Phillimore 1996.
Blake, Steven. *Cheltenham Churches and Chapels*. Cheltenham Borough Council. 1979.
Blake, Steven & Beacham, Roger.*The Book of Cheltenham*. Baracuda Books 1982.
Bradley, Clifford. *Badgeworth Church and Its Village*. 1972.
Brand, Ken. *Watson Fothergill, Architect*. For Nottingham Civic Society 1997.
Brooks, Chris & Saint, Andrew. *The Victorian Church*. The Victorian Society.
Burrow, E.J. (ed).*A Guide to The Cheltenham Ladies' College*. Cheltenham 1931.
Clarke, A.K.*The History of Cheltenham Ladies' College*. Faber. 1953.
Clarke, B.F.L. *A Study of Gothic Revival in England*. David & Charles 1969.
Colvin, H. *A Biographical Directory of English Architects*.
Cooke, Arthur. *The Forest of Dean*. 1913.
Crook, J Mordaunt. *William Burgess, The High Victorian Dream*. J Murray 1981.
Dixon, R & Muthesius, S. *Victorian Architecture*. Thames & Hudson 1978.
Douglas, J.C. *Historical Notes on Newent, Oxenhall and Pauntley*. 1912.
Faber Book of Victorian Architecture.
Gethyn-Jones, D. *Kempley: Nine Centuries of Village History*. 1957.
Gethyn-Jones, J.E. *Dymock: A History of the Church and Parish*. 1976.
Gethyn-Jones, J.E. *Kempley and Its Paintings.Vol I 1872-1958*. 1961.
Gill, Alan & Miller, Eric. *Britain in Old Postcards. Leckhampton*. Sutton Publishing 2000.
Glynne, Sir Stephen. *Gloucestershire Church Notes*. 1902.
Goding, John. *Norman's History of Cheltenham*. Cheltenham 1863.
Gray, J.E. *The Church of St Mary the Virgin, Newent*. 1962. Revised, K.M Tomlinson, 2000.
Hart, G. *A History of Cheltenham*. Leicester University Press. 1965.
Hunter, A.A. (ed) *Cheltenham College Registers, 1841-1889*.
Johnstone, J & Boothman, K. *Cheltenham Ladies' College, A Brief History & Guide*. 1996.
Jones, Anthea. *Tewkesbury*. Phillimore. 1987.
Kingsley, Nicholas. *The Country Houses of Gloucestershire Vol. I*. 1989.
Kingsley, Nicholas. *The Country Houses of Gloucestershire Vol. II*. Phillimore 1992.

Kingsley, Nicholas & Hill, Michael. *The Country Houses of Gloucestershire Vol. III.* Phillimore 2000.
Kirby, I & Torode, B. *St Stephen's Church*, Cheltenham. 1973.
Little, Bryan. *Cheltenham.* Batsford 1952.
Lowton, N. *Cheltenham College Chapel.* Cheltonian Society 1996.
Miele, Chris. *The Restoration of Victorian Churches.* The Victorian Society.
Miller, E. *The History of Leckhampton Church.* 1987.
Mowl, Tim. *Cheltenham Betrayed.* Redcliffe Press 1995.
Nicholls, H.G. *Personalities of the Forest of Dean.* 1863.
Norman, George. *The Provincial Grand Lodge of Gloucestershire.* 1911.
Paget, Mary. (ed) *A History of Charlton Kings.* CK Local History Society 1989.
Pakenham, Simone. *Cheltenham. A Biography.* Macmillan. 1971.
Pearce, Tim. *Then and Now.* The Cheltonian Society 1991.
Pooley, Charles, FSA. *Old Crosses of Gloucestershire.* London 1868.
Raikes, Elizabeth. *Dorothea Beale.* Constable. 1908.
Ralph, E & Cobb, P. *New Anglican Churches in Nineteenth Century Bristol.* University of Bristol 1991.
Royal Commission on Historic Monuments. *English Hospitals, 1660-1948.* RCHM England.
Rigby, F.F. *To Our Lady of Bromsberrow.* 1970.
Royal Institute of British Architects. *The Directory of British Architects.* 1993.
Sampson, A. *Scene Together.* Windrush Press 1992.
Sawyer, J. *Cheltenham Parish Church.* Norman Sawyer & Co. Cheltenham 1903.
Scotland, N. (ed) *A Gloucestershire Gallery.* Cheltenham 1993.
Steadman, F.C. *In The Days of Miss Beale.* Burrow. 1931.
Temple, J.A. *Woolstone And Its Church.* Folkestone. 1922.
The Church at the Crossroads. Holy Apostles Church 2000.
Verey, D, in *Pevsner's Buildings of England The Vale and the Forest of Dean.* Penguin.
Verey, D & Brooks, A, in *Pevsner's Buildings of England, The Cotswolds.* Penguin 1999.
West, V Sackville. *Berkeley Castle, An Illustrated Survey.* English Life Publications 1985.
Whiting, R. *Christ Church, Cheltenham, 1840-1990.* Cheltenham 1990.
Yorke, G. *Forthampton Church.* 1945.

GUIDES and DIRECTORIES

Cheltenham Annuaires & Directories, between 1840 and 1900 in Cheltenham Reference Library.
Gloucester Diocesan Magazine 1911.
Harrison's Gloucestershire Directory, 1859 & 1863.
Kelly's Directories, various as referred to in the chapter notes.
May's Guide to Cheltenham. London 1883.

JOURNALS, PERIODICALS, ARTICLES, PAMPHLETS

Bristol & Gloucestershire Archaeological Society. *Transactions Vol. X 1973.*
Charlton Kings Local History Society. Various *Journals* especially No 14.
Country Life. December 1973.
Gloucestershire Historical Studies Vol. II. Brian Smith for University of Bristol Extra Mural Studies. 1968.
Gloucestershire Notes & Queries. Vols. II, III, V.
Parish Magazine, All Saints Church Cheltenham 1885.
Royal Institute of British Architects, *Transactions 1886,* p11.
The Builder: many editions between 1840-1900.
The Building News and Engineering Journal – various as acknowledged in text.
The Church Builder Vol 20.
The Ecclesiologist: various editions 1840-1865.
The Journal 1887. Woolhope Naturalists Field Club.

LOCAL, COUNTY & NATIONAL NEWSPAPERS and PUBLICATIONS

Specific dates are given in the text notes.
The Cheltenham Chronicle & Gloucestershire Graphic; The Cheltenham Examiner; The Cheltenham Looker On; The Cheltenham Mercury; The Evesham Journal; The Gloucester Journal; The Tewkesbury Advertiser and Gazette; The Tewkesbury Register; The Times.

ARCHIVE SOURCES

Detailed references are included in the text notes.
Census Returns; Cheltenham Borough Archives on deposit at Gloucestershire Archives; Cheltenham Borough Archives Register of New Buildings; Cheltenham College Archives; Church of England Record Centre; ICBS Files on relevant churches at Lambeth Palace Library; Diocesan Faculty Records at the Gloucestershire Archives; Family Estate Papers and Correspondence with reference to Westholme/Abbeyholme; Listed Buildings Descriptions, as acknowledged in text; Log Book for Christ Church Schools, Cheltenham; The Middleton File at Bowes Museum, Barnard Castle; The Middleton File at Gloucestershire Archives D2970; The Middleton Files at the RIBA; Minute Books of Friends In Council; Parish Log Book for All Saints Church Cheltenham; Dunraven Diaries at The Public Record Office of Northern Ireland, Belfast,; relevant Estate Agents' Files at the Gloucestershire Archives; Relevant Parish Files at the Gloucestershire Archives.

ACKNOWLEDGEMENTS

The following individuals, organisations and departments have been of tremendous help and encouragement during the years that I have been researching John Middleton. I hope that they will accept this public recognition as my sincere gratitude for all that they have contributed towards the content of this book, although I accept full responsibility for any inaccuracies and omissions that may come to light:

The late Mrs Joy Adamson; Mr. J Askew; Roger Beacham; the late Christopher Bishop RIBA; Dr. Steven Blake; the late Miss L Eveille; Mike Grindley; Elaine Heaseman; Mrs C Leighton; the Very Reverend Allan Maclean; Geoffrey North; Miss Audrey Schuster; the late Dr. Nigel Temple; Mrs Jill Waller.

The staff at the Cheltenham Reference Library; the staff at GloucestershireArchives; the staff at the former Gloucester Library, Local Studies Department; the staff at the Library of the RIBA, London; Sarah Medlam, and Anthony Burton of the Victoria and Albert Museum; the staff at Birmingham City Reference Library; the staff at Torquay Local Studies Library; the archivist at Cheltenham College; the clergy and churchwardens who have made themselves available on my visits to churches.

The CHELTENHAM YEARS: HEREFORDSHIRE, WARWICKSHIRE and WORCESTERSHIRE

Aston, K. *Pembridge, A Walk Around the Church and Village.* C1990.

Bland, J & Hayfield, C. *Around Coleshill.* Chalford Publications.1996.

Burke & Saville. *Guide to Country Houses, Vol II Herefordshire.* 1980.

Hayfield, C & Watkins, A. *Coleshill and the Digbys.* Spring Hill Publications 1995.

Miller, E & Hayfield, C. *Coleshill Remembered.* Spring Hill Publications. 1989.

Pennant, Thomas. *Perambulations of Warwickshire.* n.d.

Pevsner, N. *The Buildings of England. Herefordshire.* Penguin.

Robinson, C. *Mansions and Manors of Herefordshire.* 1872.

Tyack, Geoff. *Country Houses of Warwickshire.* Warwickshire Local History Society. 1989.

Coleshill and Its Parish Church. 1925.

Historical Antiquities of Hereford. Hereford 1897.

The Diary of Alice Forster, courtesy of the Matron, Brockhampton Court. n.d.

DIRECTORIES

Kelly's Directory of Hereford. 1879; 1905; 1912; 1913; Littlebury's Herefordshire Directory. 1876-1877.

NEWSPAPERS

Details of references are to be found in the text notes.

The Cheltenham Examiner; The Gloucestershire Echo; The Leominster News.

ARCHIVE SOURCES

Details of references are to be found in the text notes.

GloucestershireArchives, Middleton Archive D2970; Hereford Record Office, and Worcester County Record Office; English Heritage Listed Buildings Descriptions.

ACKNOWLEDGEMENTS

Mrs Aston of Pembridge; Ms Elizabeth Lynch of Byletts; Mr Stuart Briddick formerly of Peter Hing and Jones, Architects, Birmingham, for information on Coleshill and providing access to the building prior to redevelopment; the staff of Hereford Record Office.

The CHELTENHAM YEARS: WORK in WALES

Baker-Jones, L. *Princelings, Privileges and Powers.* Gomer Publications. 1999.
Bevan, W. *St David's Diocesan History.* SPCK. 1888.
Brooks, C and Saint, A, *The Victorian Church* for the Victorian Society. 1995.
Capper, R.M. *Holy Trinity Aberystwyth-The First Hundred Years.* 1986.
Carmarthenshire Museum. *A Short History of Carmarthenshire County Museum* (Formerly Abergwili Episcopal Palace) Museum Publication. n.d.
Davies, Evan. *Hanes Plwyf Llangynllo.* 1905.
Harris, C & Startup, R. *The Church in Wales.* University of Wales Press. 1999.
Horsfall-Turner, E.R. *Walks and Wanderings in County Cardigan.* 1902.
Hughes, I; Howells, A; John, I. *St Tysul's Church, Llandysul.* 1978.
Hughes, Rev C. *A Brief History of St David's Church, Carmarthen,* 2002.
Jones, D.D. *History of Kidwelly.* 1908.
Jones, F. *Historic Cardiganshire Houses And Their Families.* Brawdy Books. 2000.
Law, Tony. *Clydey-St Clydai's Church-A History and Guide.* 1993.
Lewis, W.J. *A History of Lampeter.* Cardiganshire County Council. 1997.
Lloyd, Thomas. *The Lost Houses of Wales.* 1986.
Price, F. *History of Llansawel.* c1898.
RCAHM Wales. *Cardiganshire County History.* University of Wales Press.
RCAHM Wales. *Newport Castle, An Architectural Study.*1992.
Slater, Mike. *Old Parish Churches of S.W Wales.* Folly Publications. 1994.
Suggett, Richard. *John Nash, Architect in Wales.* 1995.
Thomas, C. Mervyn. *Cenarth Falls.* 1996.
Thomas, Rev R. *The Priory Church of St Mary Magdalene, St Clears.* 1997.
University of Wales Press. History of St David's College Lampeter. 1977.
Wallace-Hadrill, F.G. *The Parish Church of St Mary, Newport.* 1989.
Whatmore, Rev Bryan. *A Guide to St Cynllo's Church, Llangynllo.* 1998.

JOURNALS, PERIODICALS, DIRECTORIES and PAMPHLETS

Burke's *Landed Gentry* 1937.

Carmarthenshire Antiquary, various volumes acknowledged in the text notes.

Carmarthenshire Antiquarian Society, *Notes on the Older Churches in the Four Welsh Dioceses*. 1897.

Kelly's Directories, as acknowledged in the text notes.

Notes on the County Families of Cardiganshire. n.d

St Peter's Church Carmarthen. 1997

South Wales, Ancestral, Biographical and Pictorial. n.d.

The Architect, volumes acknowledged in the text notes.

The Builder, volumes acknowledged in the text notes.

The Shell Guide to Wales. 1977.

The Teifi Store 1980-1981.

West Wales Historical Records.

NEWSPAPERS

Details of references are to be found in the text notes.

The Cambrian News and Welsh Farmers' Journal; Carmarthen Journal; The Cheltenham Examiner; The Gloucestershire Echo; The Tivyside Advertiser; The Welshman.

ARCHIVE SOURCES

Without the help of the Staff of the following Agencies and Institutions, this study of the work of John Middleton in Wales would not have been as comprehensive as it is. All the original documents consulted are listed in the references at the end of the relevant chapter.

Cadw Welsh Historic Monuments, Cardiff; Cardiganshire Archives at Aberystwyth; Carmarthenshire Archives at Carmarthen; National Library of Wales, Aberystwyth; Pembrokeshire Archives at Haverfordwest; Royal Commission on the Ancient and Historical Monuments of Wales, Aberystwyth; The Local Studies' Libraries at Aberystwyth and Carmarthen.

ACKNOWLEDGEMENTS

The following persons have given freely of their time, knowledge, and research without which many of the avenues I have followed would have remained unexplored. I am indeed grateful to them as also to the many people who made themselves available to me at short notice, and in some cases invited me into their homes.

Thomas Lloyd for sharing his vast amount of research and suggesting further lines of exploration; Reverend Clive Hughes, St David's Diocesan Archivist for supplying relevant archival references for me to pursue; Julian Orbach; Mrs Vi Davies of Aberystwyth; Ken Jones, Newcastle Emlyn; Mr E. Fitzwilliams of Old Cilgwyn; Mrs Flint,

Churchwarden of Llangynllo and Malcolm Jefferies; Richard Hurlock; Mr & Mrs Holt of Newport Castle; Mr Wallace Hadrill; Fr Bryan Whatmore for permission to make use of the vast amount of research he undertook for his Llangynllo church publication; and to so many kind, friendly and helpful people of Cardiganshire, Carmarthenshire and Pembrokeshire who have been always so willing to talk, invite me into their homes, make phone calls on my behalf and help in any way that they have thought would further my research.

BIBLIOGRAPHY for JOHN HENRY MIDDLETON

Barnard, L.W. *Ninety Years Past.* Cheltenham. 1949.

Burton, Anthony. *Vision and Accident, The Story of the Victoria and Albert Museum.* V&A Publications.

Cox, Anna Somers.*The Victoria and Albert Museum: The Making of The Collection.* Windward Publishing. 1980.

Dictionary of National Biography. *Who Was Who? 1897-1916.*

Elliott, David B: *A Pre-Raphaelite Marriage. The Lives and Works of Marie Spartali Stillman & William James Stillman.* Antique Collectors' Club. 2006

Faulkner, Peter. (ed) *Jane Morris to Wilfred Scawen Blunt.* University of Exeter. 1986.

Kelvin, Norman.(ed) *The Collected Letters of William Morris.* Princeton University Press. 1984.

Lindsay, Jack. *Biography of William Morris.* New York. 1979.

Marsh, Jan & Nunn, Pamela. *Women Artists and the Pre-Raphaelite Movement.* Virago Press. 1989.

Nicholls, C.S. (ed) *Dictionary of National Biography-Missing Persons.* 1993.

JOURNALS, PERIODICALS, PAMPHLETS, ARTICLES

The Athenaeum. June 1896.

The Academy. June 1896.

The Architect and Contract Reporter. June 1896.

Bristol and Gloucestershire Archaeological Society: *Transactions,* various.

Building News. February 1890.

Proceedings of the Society of Antiquaries, London, 1895-1897.

The RIBA:*Transactions.* 1886.

LOCAL & NATIONAL NEWSPAPERS

Details of references are to be found in the text notes.

The Cambrian News; The Cheltenham Examiner; The Gloucestershire Echo; The South Wales Daily News; The Times, The Western Mail, Cardiff.

ARCHIVE SOURCES

Brookwoood Cemetery Archives, Woking; Halifax Central Reference Library, Local Studies Department; National Library of Wales, Aberystwyth, the Cilgwyn Estate Records and the Fitzwilliam Diaries;

St David's University College, Archives, Lampeter; West Yorkshire Archives Service.

ACKNOWLEDGEMENTS:

I have received tremendous help in compiling this short biography of John Henry Middleton, from Sarah Medlam at the Victoria and Albert Museum, and from her colleague, Anthony Burton, who have made available to me a vast amount of information about Middleton prior to, and during his time at the South Kensington Museum. To them both I am indeed most grateful, as I am also to the late Christopher Bishop of Daglingworth who has been a source of tremendous inspiration and guidance. I am also grateful to David Elliott, for enabling me to make contact with some of John Henry Middleton's wife's family.

I would welcome any further information, corrections or challenges about any of the people or buildings written about in this book as my Middleton file will never close.

Brian Torode. Cheltenham 2008
btsarnia@aol.com

Publisher
Accent d.o.o.
Makančeva 16
Zagreb, Croatia
www.accent.hr

Layout & Print
Denona d.o.o., Zagreb

ISBN 978-953-99762-5-3